Personal God

Also by Tim Stafford

Personal God

Can you really know the One
who made the universe?

Tim Stafford

ZONDERVAN.com/
AUTHORTRACKER
follow your favorite authors

Personal God
Copyright © 2008 by Tim Stafford

Requests for information should be addressed to:

Zondervan, *Grand Rapids, Michigan* 49530

Library of Congress Cataloging-in-Publication Data

Stafford, Tim
    Personal God : can you really know the one who made the universe?
/ Tim Stafford.
      p. cm.
   ISBN 978-0-310-27708-8
   1. Christian life. 2. God (Christianity)—Knowableness. 3. Experience
(Religion) I. Title.
BV4501.3.S725   2007
231.7—dc22   2007034456

Interior design by Beth Shagene

Printed in the United States of America

---

08 09 10 11 12 13 • 20 19 18 17 16 15 14 13 12 11 10 9 8 7 6 5 4 3 2 1

For Chase and Harriette

Contents

Foreword

Several months ago my wife and I began an experiment that is still continuing as I write. We decided to go through the listings in the Yellow Pages under "Churches" and visit every one included in our local phone book. Even though we live in a small town, we found representatives of all the major denominations and most of the minor ones as well as several unaffiliated churches, a couple of dozen congregations in all. Some have organs and choirs; most have worship bands with electric guitars and drum sets. At some, people dress up; at others they show up in blue jeans and cowboy boots. Churches meet at 7:00 a.m., 9:30, 10:30, and 11:00 a.m. on Sunday morning, a few meet on Saturday night, and one nontraditional church meets on Thursday night.

Visiting these churches, I learned to detect how "evangelical" they were almost immediately. They did not divide on the basis of theology: some individual churches in so-called liberal denominations proved quite conservative theologically, and some churches in conservative denominations seemed almost atheological and lifeless. Rather, the difference that stood out to me centered on the issue that Tim Stafford writes about in this book, the notion of knowing God personally.

I have attended churches in other countries where that notion would seem almost bizarre: a Coptic church in Egypt and an Orthodox church in Russia in which the priests speak an ancient language that no one in the congregation understands, and even a Reformation Day service in a Berlin cathedral in which the liturgy is predictable, formal, and impersonal. Evangelical churches, however, hold out the breathtaking possibility of having a direct and personal relationship with God. You can sense it in their prayers and especially in their songs, which bear a strange resemblance to the kind of love songs you hear on Top 40 radio stations — only with the words addressed to God, not to a human lover.

That the phenomenon of megachurches in the United States, let alone the dramatic growth of Christianity in many other countries, is taking place in evangelical churches points to the hunger that such a promise taps into. It is an exalted prospect that evangelicals offer, with an equally exalted potential for mis-understanding and disappointment.

Only in evangelical churches do I hear phrases like "The Lord told me ..." and "the Lord led me ..." Wor-shipers speak as comfortably and as casually of their relationship with God as they do of their relationship with family and friends. To visitors reared in a more formal church setting, not to mention agnostics and atheists, such language seems like something from an-other planet. And, as I often hear from readers who write me, such language also causes consternation even among those who earnestly seek such a personal relationship.

Books that pour forth from evangelical publishing houses often use such language without really reflect-ing on it. How, indeed, do we have a personal relation-ship with a God who spun off quasars and galaxies and who is invisible Spirit?

I have known Tim Stafford for more than three decades, and we have held many conversations on this very topic. Indeed, my own books *Reaching for the Invisible God* and *Prayer: Does It Make Any Dif-ference?* stem at least partly from some of those con-versations. No skeptic or iconoclast, Tim is a faithful follower of Jesus who has the temerity and honesty to ask questions that most of us wonder about but few of us voice aloud. I am delighted that he has now written this short, readable account of his explorations. Tim is a trustworthy guide as well as a fine writer who illustrates his ideas with poignant stories and sharp, helpful analogies.

This book does not promise one more secret that will transform your encounter with God. Rather, it takes an honest, realistic look at what may be the most important question any of us ever faces: Can we truly know God?

PHILIP YANCEY

1

A Personal Relationship
with God

Even though it was long ago, I remember the conversation perfectly. Two friends of mine were in an animated discussion. Daniel had been a sincere churchgoer all his life; Thom was a recently converted, enthusiastically born-again Christian eager to explain his faith. As the conversation proceeded, Daniel grew mildly agitated. It began to dawn on him that for all his religious involvement he was somehow not seen as truly, fully Christian.

Thom was trying to explain that Christianity is much more than good religious deeds like saying prayers and going to church. He finally blurted out, "I'm not talking about religion. I'm talking about a *personal relationship with God*!"

I knew that phrase well, for it was part of the evangelical environment I'd grown up in. That day, for the first time, I heard it the way others sometimes do, as self-confidence tipping toward arrogance: "I actually know God. He may be theory to you, but not to me."

Truly, it's a jaw-dropping claim. When you say you have a "personal relationship" with a prominent person, it means you can get to that person outside official channels; perhaps you can call him at home. Other people may know him by reputation, but you know *him*. You are not just associates; you are *friends*. Was that really what Thom meant? Did he really know the Creator of the universe *personally*?

In the classic film *Sleeper*, Woody Allen plays a Rip Van Winkle character who, after being frozen in a scientific experiment, wakes up in some distant future. He is given a stack of photographs from our times to identify. This prompts a series of hilarious one-liners. Billy Graham's picture comes up. Allen pauses, then says, "Billy Graham ... claimed to have a personal relationship with God." The audience is meant to crack up. That is how absurd the idea sounds to some.

What Did My Friend Really Mean?

I had always liked that phrase, but after listening to my friends I began to think seriously about it. What did it mean? I was convinced it did mean something, and I thought I could partly grasp its meaning by thinking of what a personal relationship was not. Perhaps Thom was trying to say that he did not relate to God institutionally, as we relate to banks or mortgage companies or the Republican Party. Or perhaps he was trying to say that he did not relate to God as a set of doctrinal propositions or as a force or as a cosmic idea.

Perhaps Thom meant that the center of the Christian faith is Jesus Christ himself, that he is a person, a man who walked and breathed and ate and talked. If we relate to God at all, it must be as one person to another—personally.

But how did Thom connect with this person Jesus? If we examined Thom's life under a microscope, minute by minute, would we be able to see it? Was there a single thing in Thom's life he could have pointed to and said, "There! That's it! You certainly·can't have *that* unless you have a personal relationship with God"?

Hungering for a Personal God

For me, this pursuit was not purely a matter of academic curiosity. I was asking these questions because I was increasingly aware of a deep hunger inside myself. I wanted to know God, to experience his presence. I did not want to "work up" a feeling of God; I wanted to encounter God directly.

During times of prayer I tried hard to convince myself that God was really listening. In one low period I walked the streets pleading with God to speak audibly, show me some sign, somehow demonstrate convincingly his presence. I didn't have to do that with my friends. They were unquestionably present. Why wasn't God?

At about that time I worked in a Connecticut restaurant washing dishes. Most of my fellow workers were Italian Americans whose version of nominal Catholicism seemed to have inoculated them against any temptation to take God or morality seriously. So a conversation with one waitress, a bone-thin divorcee with too much eye shadow, shocked me. George Harrison's song "My Sweet Lord" came on the radio in the back room. Hearing the song with its recurring words, "My sweet Lord, I really want to know you ... but it takes so long, my Lord," the waitress immediately told me of a religious experience she had had the day before. While listening to this same song, she had burst helplessly into tears. She was bewildered. "Why do you think I did that?" she demanded.

I would like to be able to say that I told her that her heart was aching for the love of Jesus, but I can't. I was as bewildered as she was. Maybe if she had been a "nice person" I would not have been so surprised at her feelings. I classed her with the tough kids I had left in high school: the boys who took auto shop and went off to join the military, and the pasty, over-made-up girls in short skirts who swore. Was it possible that such people too were hungry for God? The song moved me, but I had not expected it to move anybody else in that restaurant. And I did not know how those stirrings related to Christian faith—whether a longing that the songwriter applied to Krishna could be legitimate and not devilishly deceptive.

Later, reflecting on the experience, I began to suspect that many unlikely characters shared my longing for God. Perhaps everyone did.

God keeps popping up in people's minds. Even the anti-Christian diatribes of Richard Dawkins and Sam Harris, which are in the media spotlight as I write, suggest a preoccupation with God. What are they so bothered about? The contention that religion is behind the problems of the world strikes me as plain silly. Religion is behind the likes of Hitler, Stalin, and Mao? A belief in God is behind WWI, WWII, the Korean War, the Vietnam War, and the Iraq War? AIDS, malaria, child slavery, and global poverty exist because people believe in God?

I think the idea of God disturbs a lot of people. They find themselves longing for the meaning and comfort God could provide. Some get angry because they think the longing is hopeless. Some just feel the longing and wish they knew how to meet it.

The Big Questions

Like many others, I long for a personal God.

I grew up an evangelical Christian, and in my quest to grasp a personal relationship with God I have never quit that community. Evangelicals have many faults, not least of which is a tendency to talk glibly about God, not humbly. Still, evangelical Christianity has one quality that draws me irresistibly: it speaks openly and often about God's personal presence. I always wanted that. If religion didn't offer God at a deeply personal level, I wasn't interested.

But I still had two questions:

1. Just what could be personal about a relationship with God? Being as clear-eyed and realistically truthful as possible, what could I hope for?
2. How could I experience such a personal relationship—to really know the personal God, not just theological facts about him?

The great Roman thinker Augustine asked, "What place is there within me where my God can come? How can God come into me, God who made heaven and earth? O Lord my God, is there anything in me that can contain you?"

I want to share the answers I have found. For I have come to believe that God's personality does crowd the world around me, even inside me. I believe I can know him with the same faculties and in many of the same ways that I know my friends.

If the Bible carries one repeated message about God, it is that *he wants to be known*.

God in Everyday Reality?

Someday, Scripture says, Christians will see God face-to-face, and the sight will transform us. This historical horizon is crucial. It puts our religious experience—and our lack of it—in perspective. The apostle Paul, a man who claimed the closest personal knowledge of Jesus, wrote, *"Now* we see but a poor reflection as in a mirror; *then* we shall see face-to-face" (1 Corinthians 13:12; emphasis added).

Here and now we are not going to get all the intimacy we seek. We won't see God face-to-face. It's important to understand that.

Nevertheless, Christianity is not merely a matter of waiting for Jesus to come back to earth. It is life in everyday reality. Within that everyday reality, can we know Jesus personally?

When I first began to ask this question, I could not answer it. I could see very little that was "personal" in my ordinary Christian life of prayer and Bible study and church involvement. And my evangelical friends weren't much help. True, they talked about a personal relationship. "God led me to ..." was a common phrase. Some claimed to hear God's voice. But I never heard anyone clarify these claims. If someone said, "God led me to stop and see my friend Mary," no one asked whether God did, indeed, prompt that and how. I never heard any pastor say, "We're going to sing 'He Touched Me,' and then we'll talk about the questions it raises." Some people certainly must have had questions, but they never voiced them.

So I backed up a step. Instead of asking what a personal relationship with God might be, I asked what a personal relationship might be—*any* personal relationship. When I asked the question that way, I made a fundamental discovery: personal relationships are peculiar. They operate by a mysterious set of rules, depending on facial expressions that we can't define and knowledge that we can't explain. Engineers can make blueprints of any machine in the world, and a good machine shop can duplicate them. But you can't use a blueprint to duplicate a friendship. The most compelling reality in any of our lives—our relationships—is very hard to describe or define. We know people in a way entirely different from the impersonal way we know objects and forces and ideas.

What the phrase "personal relationship with God" claims, most basically, is that God is a person. Since I am a person, I must therefore know him through these peculiar means by which people know each other.

I admit that this does not seem, at first glance, like a very dramatic discovery. But it led me to a train of thought that has transformed my search for deeper intimacy with God.

I sometimes pose this question: Suppose a young woman is dating a man ten years older than she. Although she senses strong mutual attraction, she is not sure she really knows him. Because of their age difference he seems unlike any of her friends. How should she get to know him?

When I pose this question, people come up with a long list of ways to know others: by talking together, sharing activities, meeting each other's friends and family, exchanging life histories, reading the same books, discussing the same movies or television shows, working on a project together, and so on. Some may emphasize one way over another, but no one has ever suggested that just one of these means is all that is needed. Everyone agrees that we get to know people by experiencing them from many different angles.

Contrary to this, many spiritual programs emphasize only one avenue to God: a type of Bible study, a method of prayer, a style of social activism, a form of worship. "Do this," they seem to say, "and you will know God." They inadvertently create a mechanical image of God. If only we could get one broken piece of the machine going (speaking in tongues or yielding to God's power or reading the Bible daily or serving the poor), our spiritual life would start up and take off like a lawn mower.

Personal relationships do not work that way. They are not mechanical. They are built out of a mosaic of different experiences, most quite ordinary. Small pieces go together to make something surprising.

If you want to grow closer to someone, you usually don't look for some new, exotic approach. You look to make better use of the opportunities already at hand. "Why don't we start meeting for lunch on a regular basis?" you might say; or, "I think we need to talk about deeper things." You seek to add small pieces that are truly meaningful and deeply personal. You watch to see a bigger picture emerge.

Knowing God Is Not So Difficult

In this book, I want to explore how knowing God personally is similar to the ways we know others and know ourselves. It will take some patience as we put pieces of a mosaic together.

In doing this, there is one mistake we must not make. We must not portray knowing God as over-whelmingly difficult or complicated. It is not. The Bible tells us, again and again, that God is very near. And he is near because he wants to be near.

If God wanted to hide from us, we would play hide and seek for the rest of our lives. But God chooses to open up to each of us. God has told us to find him in prayer, in church, in Scripture, in the Lord's Supper, in following his example of sacrifice and service. These are the classic pathways, sometimes called the "means of grace." They are not a program. They are God's free and gracious offering of a relationship. He wants to know us, and to be known.

I don't have a new spiritual technique to offer. I hope to wake you up, to make you lift your head and open your eyes. Every day God holds himself out to us, asking to be known. His personality spills over into the details of daily life—in the morning's sunshine that he handcrafts every day, in the kindness of a friend's smile—and even in and through the humdrum ordinariness of most church services. If you can begin to see that God is available not as some "power" or "holiness" but as *himself*, I think you will pursue a relationship with clearer eyes and greater hope. Your longing can begin to be filled. The one who made the universe is inviting you to enter a personal relationship.

2

Introductions
on a First-Name Basis

Every personal relationship begins in the same way: we exchange names.

We forget how strange this is. Smiling at you, I utter a short sound that has no meaning in English. You eagerly take it up, repeating it to be sure it sticks in your memory. You may comment if you like its sound. Then, in exchange, you utter a similarly meaningless sound, which I must remember.

Why do we perform this ritual? Names help with identification, as do license plates on cars. But there is much more in a name than identification; otherwise we could exchange Social Security numbers. We do not like it when computers reduce us to numbers, and we would be outraged if people did. Numbers are impersonal; names are personal.

Even in a crowded, noisy room we can pick out our names spoken. Names are personalized combinations of sounds that belong to us. They are passwords offering access to our personality.

Sometimes names convey important information. In some cultures they reflect birth order, phases of the moon, or the day of the week when you were born.

My full name is Timothy Chase Stafford. Stafford is my father's family name, and presumably I could trace it back to England, to Staffordshire, and to some shallow spot in a river where you could cross with a staff in hand. Chase is my grandmother's maiden name—you could trace that back too. Timothy reflects various Timothys my parents knew and most significantly the Timothy of the New Testament. By my name alone you can prove that I am not an isolated individual but part of a vast family tree spreading out through space and time—to England and to Palestine. A kind of immortality speaks through names, a perpetuation of beloved people through their children and grandchildren and even their friends' children. (You can hardly give a handsomer compliment than naming your child after a friend.)

Still, the names themselves are often meaningless. What makes "Bob" or "Jane"—such short, plucky syllables—into names? When I was in grade school, a teacher who had taught briefly in Turkey told us some of her students' names. We laughed incredulously. To us these did not sound like names at all. No doubt the students in Turkey would have said the same thing about our names.

Names are mysterious. Yet we must exchange names to have a relationship.

The exchange of names seems to have no functional value. I can carry on business at a bank or an office for a long time without exchanging names. I have been trading at the same grocery store for more than twenty years, and I know at least a dozen of the clerks by sight. We have a friendly and efficient relationship. It is not what I would call a personal relationship. They have been trained to address me as "Mr. Stafford" after looking at my receipt; I could address them by name by checking their nametags. But that is an artificial familiarity. We both know we are there for business: I want groceries; they want a paycheck. It is a great arrangement. But it is not a personal relationship.

In some restaurants the waiter greets you by saying, "Hi! My name is Angie, and I'll be your server tonight." But she never says, "Hi! My name is Angie! What's yours?" She tells me her name to create an atmosphere of casual friendliness, but everybody knows it is fictional. This is not a personal relationship. Not really. It is a business relationship. If Angie asked me my name, she would be understood to be suggesting something more.

We exchange names when we want a personal relationship. It is nearly impossible, not to say unbearable, to carry on a personal relationship for any length of time while not knowing each other's names. The urge is almost overpowering to offer your own little syllables and ask your newfound friend for his. When you do so, you make an overture of friendship. By your simple action you say, "I would like us to know each other."

God Introduces Himself

How amazing, therefore, to discover that God introduces himself by name. Why would a god do that? If you think of the great Hindu gods—Krishna or Vishnu or Ganesh—you can't imagine them coming down to our level and staying there, relating like an ordinary person. Or consider the Greek gods—Aphrodite, Apollo, Zeus. What do they care about human beings that they should want to form a personal relationship? Gods are above and beyond us. That is what makes them gods.

The God of the Bible, however, is different. True, when he calls Moses from the burning bush he seems shrouded in mystery, telling Moses to take off his shoes because the ground he is walking on is holy. But then God does the unthinkable. He introduces himself. He tells Moses the name he answers to: Yahweh.

Yahweh is not a regular word with a regular meaning. It draws on the root of "to be," so that some people translate it "I am." But God is not making a speech about his nature. He is introducing himself. Yahweh is a name, like Tim or Judy.

The God who spoke from the burning bush wanted to convince Moses that he cared—that he was concerned for him and his relatives on a personal level, that he was attuned to their suffering. And more: God wanted an ongoing personal relationship with the people of Israel. He wanted to personally accompany them out of Egypt. That is why he told Moses his name.

Unfortunately most Bible translations turn God's very personal name into something impersonal, "Lord" or "Lord God," which is more a title than a name. There would be nothing remarkable in addressing God as "Lord." Everybody in the Middle East knew enough to call the gods "Lord." By introducing himself as Yahweh, God was giving a unique and personal name by which only his friends could address him.

Ironically, the Israelites came to respect God's name so much they would never actually say it. They substituted euphemisms, such as "the Name above all Names." Because it was such an awesome invitation to intimacy, Yahweh became a forbidden word. By an odd quirk of human nature, God's most personal overtures are often turned into things so holy and rarefied that they end up quite impersonal.

That was not God's intent. By giving his name, God says clearly, I want to have a personal relationship. I am introducing myself. I am telling you my name so that you can call me.

God did this to let the Israelites know he would be very near, personally protecting them, putting out food for them every night and setting up signposts for their journey every day. He was not just the great God of the universe. He was their own personal God, who cared. He would go with them on their dangerous trip to Palestine.

For us, God's name means much the same thing. I mentioned that a person can pick out his name even if it is said in a crowded, noisy room. So with God. Amid the incredible clatter of the universe, the motion and clamor of billions, when we speak his name, God tunes in. We have his attention when we call out to him. He will keep a close eye on us. He will stay close to us all through our dangerous journey.

Other Names of God

If Moses' story were the end of the story, we might want to go back to addressing God as Yahweh, the way the Psalms do. (Most of the time when the psalmist says,

"Lord," the word is "Yahweh" in the original Hebrew.) We don't need to do that because God has given us an even better, more personal name: Jesus.

"Jesus" was a very common Jewish name. It is actually a rendering of "Joshua," the famous Old Testament hero who led the Israelites into Palestine, their promised home. In Jesus' time this was a name like "Anthony" or "William" in ours. Lots of Jewish boys were named "Jesus." As such, the name Jesus communicates even more powerfully than "Yahweh" that God wants to relate to us at a human level.

My wife's name, "Popie," is a rather odd name she acquired in childhood. It is dear to me because she is dear to me. Her name has become part of who she is. Likewise, the name "Jesus" becomes meaningful because it is attached to a real human being. We know about Jesus. We know his life story and we know his reputation. When we address God as "Jesus" all the Gospels come tumbling out of our mouths, as do all Jesus' actions through the Holy Spirit in the years since he walked on earth.

Millions of Christians mumble the phrase "in the name of Jesus" at the end of their prayers, as though those words give a special boost of power to their words. They miss the point. "In the name of Jesus" is not an incantation. It is a reference to a person we have the privilege to know personally.

As a writer, I'm sometimes approached by friends who want my help in contacting a publisher. Often I'll suggest someone they should call, and I'll say, "Use my name." When we pray "in the name of Jesus" it means we have a connection. We are not just speaking words into the mystery. We are speaking on the recommendation of a person whom we know, who has introduced us to himself and said, "Use my name." That is an intensely personal connection.

The Most Personal Name of All

Even the name of Jesus, as personal as it is, gets trumped by yet a third name. Jesus taught us to speak to God as "Father." In itself, "Father" is not a name at all, but a title. Only one small group uses "Father" as a name—the Father's children.

People call me on the phone; people email me. They address me as "Tim" or "Mr. Stafford." I try to give each person my respectful attention. One address, though, always has my complete interest: "Dad."

When we say, "Our Father," we are instantly transported to a private setting, where families talk. The children address their father by this name, and they have an exclusive corner on his attention and his love.

Children may wander off from their father, as did the prodigal son, but the father cannot forget his children if he is any kind of father at all. To be a father is to be irrevocably committed.

When we say, "Our Father," we are calling on God the way Jesus did. The two of them were so close that Jesus could say, "I and the Father are one." When Jesus taught us to pray, "Our Father," he had in mind his own intimate, personal privilege of family. This name clearly goes beyond a mere introduction.

We human beings have an innate longing to know God, our Creator. We crave this the way abandoned children yearn to know their fathers. The hunger for relationship goes deep.

If Jesus is right and God really does welcome our addressing him as "Father," we have come upon a most stunning fact: we can relate to God as members of the family. The door is open to the most profoundly personal relationship—that of a child to a parent.

Who Says There Is a Personal Invitation?

We learn about God's invitation from the Bible, which describes how God introduces himself as Yahweh, as Jesus, and as Father. He could, of course, introduce himself the way aliens do in science fiction movies—with brilliant lights, fast-moving clouds, loud noises. Indeed, he sometimes did something like that in the Old Testament. For us, though, he makes his invitation through an old book, a classic.

I would make the case that the Bible is the best possible way for God to offer relationship. I don't deny that a mystical experience might *feel* better. But would it accomplish what is needed? A relationship with God is not like just any relationship. God is invisible. God is impossibly beyond our understanding. A personal relationship with him is bound to be difficult and subject to doubt.

Imagine yourself meeting a Very Important Person —a president, a movie star, a world-famous author. She glances at you, then focuses her gaze on your eyes. "I want to get to know you," she says. "Call me." And then she is gone.

Such a stunning invitation! Even if it proved difficult to connect again with the Very Important Person —as it surely would—you might persevere as you remembered that look in her eyes. But doubts would surely come in. Did you hear correctly? (Most people would think you dreamed it.) Was she just kidding? Maybe that was her standard line, lacking any authentic follow-through. It would be much easier to keep pursuing a relationship if she sent you a note.

An invitation to relationship with God is too significant to leave to transitory visions, experiences that can be reexamined and doubted the next day, conversations that leave no tangible evidence that they ever happened. If God were really determined to invite a whole group of people, indeed the whole world, into personal relationship, he ought to make a formal and written record of it. He should engrave such an invitation in gold-embossed letters on fine rag paper. And so he has. You can read it in the Bible. Anybody can read it. It does not change. The invitation is permanent.

Put another way, God's invitation leaves behind the strictly personal and mystical, entering the realm of history. God really spoke to Moses, sharing his name, and the event was recorded as a public document. God really approached us in Jesus, who really taught his followers to address God as "Father." Jesus' life and teachings were written down by eyewitnesses and carefully preserved for us. God really has broken into history and made himself available for personal relationship. The invitation is factual and historical. You can look it up.

The Fear of Rejection

If God has approached with such a personal invitation, only one response is appropriate. You jump in eagerly. You begin to relate.

But some people are fearful. A friend of mine, whom I'll call Marie, married a man from another race.

She knew her father didn't approve, but she hoped he would get over it.

Marv really was a wonderful man: kind, hardworking, idealistic, gentle. For many years Marv and Marie lived overseas, serving poor people in tough, deprived environments. As a pair they made a marvelous team, and those who knew them loved them. Together they had three beautiful children.

But Marie's father did not come around. He refused to talk to Marie, let alone Marv. He even refused to acknowledge his grandchildren.

Marie kept trying to reconcile. It hurt deeply to be rejected by her own father, but she would reach out to him in ways she thought he could accept. He never acknowledged her efforts, always rebuffing her instead. Once, in desperation, she took her young son to her father's door. He opened it, saw her and the child, and slammed the door in their faces.

Some people fear that kind of treatment from God. They approach him with a sense of foreboding. They're expecting rejection, guilt, recrimination. Afraid to become hopeful and vulnerable, they expect to find the door slammed in their faces.

It is an understandable fear, but the Bible says they have it the wrong way round. We are not at God's door, knocking. Rather, God stands outside *our* door, asking to come in (Revelation 3:20). He has offered relationship, introducing himself. Now he waits for a response.

"I revealed myself to those who did not ask for me ... I said, 'Here am I, here am I.' All day long I have held out my hands to an obstinate people" (Isaiah 65:1–2). If it is strange to find God introducing himself, this is doubly strange: God parked outside your door, waiting on you to open up.

If you want a personal relationship, God has done everything to make it possible. You have only to open the door, to say come in.

I Want a Relationship

People usually open that door of relationship by prayer. To the invisible God they simply say, "Come in. I want a relationship. I'm sorry for what I've done in the past to keep you outside. I want to give up everything that keeps you out of my life. I want to know you."

If nobody is out there, of course, you will open the door and get no response. But if God is real, and his invitation is real, you will have started on something with profound implications for your life. Started, I say. Remember that hardly any relationship seems profound when you are first introduced.

The beginning matters hugely, though. As the saying has it, a journey of a thousand miles begins with a single step. We even have a ceremony to mark that first step called baptism. Baptism makes a public declaration that both you and God are committed to the relationship. Baptism can have a powerful effect in the same way that a marriage ceremony can have a powerful effect, sealing your commitment.

If you accept God's offer of a personal relationship, if by prayer you invite him into your life, if you participate in baptism at your church, it remains true that none of this will necessarily seem real. Some people feel exhilarated and sure right from the beginning, but not all. You may feel as though you are just acting out a charade, going through the motions of relating to God just like you did with an Invisible Friend when you were young.

Those kinds of feelings are common enough. Lots of people feel that way on their wedding day too—that they are just acting a part. It doesn't seem real.

How do you know whether it is real—that you are not just fooling yourself? The proof of reality lies in what follows.

3

Talking to God

You have been introduced. You have exchanged names. You have begun a relationship. Now what? The answer is obvious: you talk.

In conversation we reveal our thoughts, our inner selves. We learn about each other's past. We exchange ideas and dreams. We laugh. No relationship ever goes beyond the superficial or the impersonal without plenty of talking.

But how is this possible with God? Deep in our hearts we long to know him, and we feel a natural impulse to carry on a conversation with him. New believers may think that they should use dressed-up "holy" language to address God, but most soon realize that's not really true to themselves. They want to talk with God, to know him and be known, just as they do in other personal relationships. That is the main reason people pray, even if they have doubts. (The other reason is that they are desperate, and they hope God can help.)

Do they really get what they are hoping for? People say, "God spoke to me," but when you press the point you usually find that they mean it metaphorically. Maybe once or twice in a lifetime—if that—they hear an audible voice. Most people, most of the time, get at most a feeling, an impression of what God might think. That is fine, but can it be the basis for a personal relationship? Imagine befriending someone who speaks only a few words over the course of a lifetime. What kind of relationship can you have?

There is no point pretending that a relationship with God is just like other relationships. He is God, and it would be unreasonable to think that we can befriend him the way we do anyone else. The question is, can we carry on an exchange of words—a conversation—that genuinely draws us into an ongoing personal relationship?

Asking for Change

I want to start with the form of prayer that most people think of first, even though other aspects of prayer may be more important to personal relationship. Let us start with the kind of prayer that asks God to do things.

With my fellow human beings, I can have a relationship without making requests. I might meet you every week for coffee and become very close, even though I never once asked you for a favor.

I do not think this is possible with God, however. At least, I cannot imagine it. Can a little child relate to his parents without ever asking for anything? If I can really talk to the Creator of the universe, whose amazing power can shape everything to his design, then it would be astonishing if I didn't ask him to do something. The world is really not so neat that I can accept it as it is.

What kind of relationship with God would fail to notice injustice, sickness, war, sadness, and poverty, the very matters that the God of the Bible claims to care about? And not just to notice them, but to ask him to do something about them?

I have to talk with him about the AIDS epidemic. I have to tell him about my friends who are struggling to keep their marriage together. I have to talk about Darfur, Iraq, Sri Lanka, or wherever else innocent people are suffering in the ferocity of war. I have to ask him to heal my friend who is suffering in the grip of cancer.

Asking God to do things is an inescapably natural impulse, and God encourages it. The Bible tells us to request what we need and what others need. Yet we know, all the same, that we can't really tell God anything new. He knows all about AIDS, strained marriages, Darfur, and our friends with cancer. He knows everything that we know and more. Furthermore, he already has plans for the world—better plans than we can come up with. We assume that nothing we say can make him do what he doesn't want to do. (If God is as good as we think he is, we would never want him to do what he doesn't want to do.)

So why should we ask? What are we doing telling him what he already knows and asking him to take action in ways he already intends to?

Asking God for help makes no sense until we realize that his perspective is so very different from ours. The problems of war and disease and family breakdown are overwhelming to us, beyond our power, and so we turn to God urgently seeking his powerful help. We want action above all else.

God has to see it differently. He is the highest power in the universe, hotter than the sun, stronger than gravity. Miracles are easy for him. He does not worry about getting things done. He can cure cancer or end war without even bending over.

His preoccupation is with something apparently more difficult, something that his power is helpless before. He wants us to share his mind. He seeks communion. And he cannot force that.

That is why he makes our requests so important. If we don't approach him with our concerns, he waits. He could fix things without us, but he would rather stay quiet until we join him. When at long last we come to him with our concerns, we take the first step into what he most seeks: communion between creature and Creator, who join in partnership toward the reconciliation of all things. This is his priority, above all else.

A Startling Responsibility

If that is how it is, then prayer is a startling responsibility. Not just our own welfare depends on it; the welfare of the world is in our hands. God is waiting for us to care.

God chooses to depend on us. He waits for our fickle attention to focus on the things that need doing. He is willing to let our apathy or inattention interfere with healing, with reconciliation, with joy he wants to bring. All kinds of disasters may occur without his involvement because he does not have our attention—we do not care enough to pray.

It is a great humiliation for God to wait on us. In his first humiliation he came to earth, limiting himself to flesh and blood in order to reach us. Now he goes further down, limiting himself to our weak attentions.

So when I go to pray for my friend with cancer, I try to expunge any idea that I am bringing the matter to God. Rather, I try to remember that God is already there. I am not asking him to join me in my concern. I am joining him. He has been waiting for me—waiting to act and to help until I am there with him. He has never, not for an instant, taken his eyes off my friend. Perhaps God would like to ask me a question: "What took you so long?" Or "Why aren't you here more often?"

Not that God will necessarily do my bidding, just as I express it. It would be shocking to think of God as someone who wants nothing better than what I want. Of course he sees far deeper than I do. Of course he wants much better results than I can even imagine.

He is not, we devoutly hope, guided strictly by our requests. Why he sometimes does what we ask and not other times we cannot say. We can only conclude that he knows more than we do about what should be done.

Still, we are bound to get it right sometimes. (And more often, I hope, as we live a long time in relationship to him and learn his ways, living and praying by faith.) As you speak to him about your concerns and worries, I think you will notice that (often quietly and invisibly) he makes things right. Wars do end. Marriages mend. Cancers disappear. These wonders do not happen as quickly or as often as we wish, but they do happen when we pray.

People sometimes say that prayer works wonders. I do not think this is quite correct. God works wonders. Prayer lets us participate in these and draws us into closer relationship with him.

What I Say to Myself

Our requests, then, make sense within a larger framework of God seeking relationship with us. Not all our prayers are requests, though. There is praise. There is lament. There is confession.

Do these kinds of prayer make sense? As I mentioned, God already knows everything I have to say before I even open my mouth. He knows what I feel. He knows whether I love and adore him. Why should I tell him anything when he already knows it all? How can that further a relationship?

Consider this, however: I talk all the time to someone who already knows everything about me. I'm a little embarrassed by it, but I talk to myself. Sometimes I talk out loud. More often I keep my thoughts silent, not wanting people to think I'm crazy. Still, all day long I carry on a running discussion with myself. I replay events that have happened, especially emotional incidents. I remind myself what I need to do. I express faith in myself: "You can do this." I urge myself on: "Get down to it. No more wasting time!"

Sometimes I rebuke myself: "Why did you take a second helping? You need that bowl of ice cream like you need an extra stomach!" Often I coach myself: "Try to be friendly. Nobody is going to chop your head off." Nor do I forget to praise: "You were good! All right!"

Why do I talk to myself this way? I am certainly not communicating information. I can't tell myself anything that I don't already know. And yet, self-talk really does seem to perform an important function in my life. It raises issues into conscious consideration so I can reach harmony with myself over them. It helps me to get myself together.

The Way Old Friends Talk

One wouldn't want to overemphasize this in talking about God, because, after all, "me" and "myself" are the same person. Thinking about how I talk to myself does remind me, however, that good communication doesn't always mean communicating new information. Just because I already know everything doesn't mean that there's nothing important to say.

The best example of this is the way I talk in my closest relationships. The more intimate our friendship, and the more frequently we are together, the less "news" we have to tell each other. And yet we have more, not less, to say.

I think particularly of my wife. Of course, we communicate a lot of news on a day-to-day basis. But since we're together every day, most of the news isn't very big. Truthfully, a lot of our communication has a very low information content. Yet we never run out of things to say. We talk about our kids—a subject we've covered so thoroughly and so often I can almost tell what Popie will have to say before she says it. Often neither one of us is really looking for a response. "I've been thinking about Katie," she says. "Yeah, me too," I add. "I really love that girl," she says. "Mmmm," I opine.

What exactly is the point of this conversation? Yet truthfully, these are the types of conversations that have the most meaning for us both. We stand side by side looking at the same object. We are drawn together by our shared concern, our shared love, our shared worry.

Sometimes our words may lead one of us to take action. More often, joining together in concern is enough. With God it is the same: we talk to him not mainly because he needs our advice on how to run the world, or because he lacks our knowledge and insight into how things are. We talk to God so we can be close.

In my conversations with Popie we encourage each other with praise and thanks. Again, it's usually nothing new. I know Popie admires and loves me. Yet I need to hear it from her. Even in areas where I feel complete self-confidence, I want her affirmation. It draws us together. Other times I must confess to her that I am sorry for something I have done, some unnecessary harsh word or careless act. My repentance is not really news to her. She knows I am sorry, and I know that she will forgive me. Yet the words need to be said because only as I make myself vulnerable to her can we enter into communion again.

With old friends we talk about our pasts because we find intense pleasure in reliving memories and shared moments. "Remember when ..." We exchange our views not because our old friends will be surprised, but precisely because they will not. We draw an intense, familiar enjoyment in hearing predictable opinions from someone we love. "I knew you would say that. You haven't changed a bit!"

Old friends are like old dogs lying in the sun — just being together and sharing the same sunlight is wonderful. Dogs, however, miss out on the full joy; they cannot talk about it. I say to my wife, "Doesn't the sun feel wonderful?" and, "This reminds me of the sun porch we had in Palo Alto." I say nothing new, and she does not really need to respond. It is almost as though I were talking to myself. But the words and her listening ear draw us into communion.

Here, I believe, is the fundamental clue to understanding conversation with God. When we raise our concerns to God, we stand by him and look with him toward people and problems that we care about mutually. When we turn our eyes toward him, we say out loud our love and appreciation, just as we look toward our oldest and dearest friends and tell them how we care for them, though they already know it. We confess to God what we are and what we have done, which he knows all about. We express our faith in him. We thank him for who he is and what he has done for us. None of this is news to him, but all of this draws us together.

Talking to God Is Communion

Crucially, then, we need to learn to talk to God as frequently as we talk to ourselves, as freely as we talk to our most intimate friends. If you want a close personal relationship with God, leave nothing out of the conversation. Tell him of your preoccupations, worries, hopes, and concerns. Share your passion, anger, and humor. Talk to God all day long. When you lie awake at night, talk to him. When you wake up in the morning, greet him and go over your plans for the day together. In the car on your way to work, turn down the radio and talk to him. When you are angry, frustrated, or worried, explain why to him. When you are happy, share it with him. Open up. If you happen to find yourself talking to yourself, shift to telling God about the same subject. He wants to hear. You will begin to experience communion with God as you do this.

4

God Talking Back

I hope I have convinced you that there is a point in speaking to God, and the point is precisely personal relationship. What about the other side? Does God speak back? Does he answer prayer, not just in the sense of doing what we request, but in actually responding to us with words?

Getting answers to your prayers is not enough. A machine does things at your request. Put a dollar in a vending machine and you will get something out. Only a friend, though, will talk to you about what troubles you or offer advice as you ponder your life direction.

If God does not speak to us, then our hope of personal relationship is in trouble. If we speak but get no response, then perhaps God is just an Imaginary Friend—a way for us to comfort ourselves.

It is important to avoid being glib. Despite the inflated claims some Christians make, God does not habitually speak to his friends in anything like the way another person would.

We would like God to break into our consciousness with a direct message. We would prefer an audible voice, if possible. We wish God communicated in the way our friends do. He can. In the Bible there are many accounts of God in direct communication—sometimes appearing in a vision or a dream, sometimes speaking audibly in a voice that could be mistaken for thunder.

Direct messages are different from the inner impressions that people sometimes report by saying, "I feel the Lord is leading me to ..." In the Bible nobody says, "I *feel* that the Lord is telling me to do something." When God spoke, they had no doubt about whom they were hearing. They could only choose whether or not to trust and obey God's voice. Angels and visions and dreams and voices that brought God's word were indisputably foreign to the minds that received them. If this kind of voice speaks to you, I think you will know it.

Personally, I have not had that kind of communication. But I know people who have. I know a man who was sitting in his car at a stop light when he felt a kind of burning on the left side of his face and heard a very clear inner communication that he should begin to pray for the pastors of the church on the corner immediately to his left, pastors whom he envied and resented. When this man describes his experience, I find him convincing. I'm quite confident he is not making it up or indulging in exaggeration.

A friend of mine went through a heartbreaking marriage and divorce. She became a Christian in the middle of that awful experience, which helped heal many of the wounds she suffered. But as she grew toward middle age she realized that she might never remarry and, even more painfully, might never have children.

Then one day in prayer she had a very powerful and clear communication from God: she should make room for children.

She is not somebody who gets words from God. But this was so clear she told her friends about it, asking them to hold her accountable to obey it. Where children would come from she had no idea.

She began applying to adopt. How would this work? Not only was she single, she was a special-education elementary school teacher in the inner city. She had a very clear idea of how difficult single motherhood would be because she had seen so many single mothers at her school. She was completely certain, however, that God had spoken to her. So she kept going.

One of her prayer partners was worried. Adopting a child would be disastrous for her friend, she thought, so she asked another friend, in another city, to pray. The friend she called said, "Oh." Taking out a copy of her church directory, she cut out the picture of a man.

His wife had died of cancer a year ago. He had two little girls and was completely overwhelmed. She sent the picture to her friend. They did some matchmaking. And the result was a marriage—one of the most wonderful marriages I know.

These are some of my best friends. I have watched those two little girls grow up into young women. Do I believe that God speaks? I do.

Still, by every reliable account, that kind of communication is unusual. It might happen once or twice in a lifetime to some. God rarely says, "Join this committee" or "Move to Colorado" in an audible or unquestionable way.

Actually, he rarely spoke that way in the Bible. The times he did are reported, naturally. But don't overlook the much more frequent times when he evidently did not. He told the apostle Paul in a vision, "Come over to Macedonia." But that was virtually the only time when he guided Paul by such a direct message. All Paul's other travels appear to be guided by more mundane considerations, such as whom he needed to see and what problems cried out to be addressed. No direct messages.

The book of Acts describes a terrible conflict over what kind of behavior to expect from non-Jewish believers. It was arguably the most important moment in the history of the early church. At stake was the question of whether Christianity would become a global religion or would remain a Jewish sect. A special council met in Jerusalem to decide the issue, and sharply different perspectives were offered.

How were they to decide? No voice from heaven spoke to God's people. No one stood up to say, "God told me ..." The issue was decided on the basis of what they had observed God doing (Acts 15:8–9), on their own experiences (Acts 15:10–11), and on the Old Testament Scriptures (Acts 15:15–18).

You will operate that way too, most of the time. You will not often get direct answers to the questions you pose to God. What you will get, as you immerse yourself in his Word and live with him in prayer, is a deeper sense of walking with him, living with him, talking with him, and being directed by him. There will be a kind of conversation in your constant praying and his constant revealing of himself and his will.

It can be very intimate, though not all the time. Personal relationships are like that. I do not feel close to my wife all the time, but we always have a personal relationship and we are always growing together because we live in communion and we talk.

The Bible and the Voice of God

The Bible is at the heart of God's speaking. It is, at one level, just a book—a historical record of God's involvement with the human race. It includes extensive accounts of what God himself said, often through the voice of his prophets, especially his prophet and Son, Jesus. Some Bibles print Jesus' words in red because these particular words record God's audible voice.

The claim that the Bible is God's Word reaches far wider than that, though. The Bible does not merely include God's words; it is, as a whole, God's Word. That is because it gives a well-rounded and completely reliable portrait of who God is, what he wants, what he hates, and what he is doing. The Bible is what God wants you to know about him. He inspired its creation so that you could get to know him.

The Bible focuses on areas where God's life intersects with our lives. It does not tell many stories of what happens in heaven, and it mostly leaves the inner workings of the Trinity to our imagination. The same with God's relation to Satan and his interactions with angels, God's spirit messengers. These are important areas, no doubt, which some people find intensely interesting. Scripture, though, focuses its light on interactions between God and human beings, and it shows God passionately involved in these relationships.

Regarding your own personal relationship with God, however, you might say, "So what?" What you read in the Bible are other people's relationships, not yours. Besides, the Bible is a very ancient book. Hardly anybody today has an older book in their library. Not a word has changed in almost two thousand years. Does this word speak to *me*? Is it personal?

The answer must be, "Not necessarily." It is quite possible to read Scripture as an ancient curiosity, the way most ancient books are read—the Babylonian *Epic of Gilgamesh*, Livy's *History of Rome*, Euripides' *The Cyclops*. Such ancient books come from another era and another place. In such books the characters speak, sometimes powerfully, but they do not speak to us.

Many people read the Bible that way. They may read it for information about ancient Hebrew religion, for theological propositions, for the beauty of its language, or for inspiration. They may find it soothing. But for them it is not personal.

The Personal Voice at the Heart of Scripture

Something has to happen in order for this ancient book to speak personally to us. This "something" is the Holy Spirit.

Who is the Holy Spirit? The simplest answer is that he is God or, to be more exact, God-with-us. When we invite God to begin a personal relationship with us, the Holy Spirit is the one who answers.

And here is one very important way he answers our invitation. He takes the impersonal record of Scripture and makes it speak personally to us. When we read words of encouragement and comfort in the Bible, we hear them as encouragement and comfort directed from God to us—personally, in our unique circumstances. When we read words of warning, we hear them directed to us as clearly as we heard our mother's warning voice when we were young. The words of Scripture are the same words we once read impersonally, and we understand them using the same intellectual tools that we would use to understand any book. Yet they speak to us directly and personally as God, through the Holy Spirit, speaks them to us. Because of this, the words are transformed. It is all the difference between reading Dear Abby's advice column every day and reading her column on the day she answers your letter. The advice is the same but it is directed to you.

Such personal communication doesn't necessarily happen every day. Sometimes, maybe often, the Bible is just a useful and interesting book. As you live in relationship to God, though, you find that it speaks in another voice to you more and more, the voice of a loving God.

This is true both in a particular and a general sense. Much of what the Bible communicates comes in discrete messages: a word of encouragement, a word about God's glory, a word of moral guidance. Through the Holy Spirit, those words become unavoidably personal, directed to you. You read them and you know they apply to your situation. God speaks to you through them.

At the same time, the Bible communicates a general message about God's involvement with the human race, beginning with Adam and Eve and romping down through the millennia. Through the Holy Spirit, I learn how to understand my own story as fitting into this big story. Even if I don't comprehend all the details, I gain an increasing sense that God has a plan for my life that fits into his plan. To make an analogy, I am like an American soldier on the night before D-Day, who somehow is given a copy of General Eisenhower's detailed strategy for the invasion of Normandy. Perhaps that soldier had no idea until that moment why he has been trained to storm ocean cliffs. Now he understands perfectly—and he understands how much is at stake in his performance.

As I absorb God's Big Story, reading it over and meditating on it, I begin to grasp why I have been given certain gifts and privileges and experiences. The pieces of my life begin to fit together—not perfectly, but significantly—and I feel it as the personal involvement of my God, who holds all the keys to my life. As I read the story of his work on earth, I understand increasingly that I am reading my own story. God is explaining to me who I am and what he wants from me.

This witness of the Holy Spirit through the Bible is the fundamental way that God communicates with us. It doesn't have the immediacy of human conversation. I don't ask God questions and get immediate responses. The conversation is muted and requires patient listening. There are long silences—sometimes very frustrating silences. It is very personal, however. It brings us closer and closer together because I understand more of his mind and heart while I share more of my own with him. When I am stymied or in trouble, I listen for God's voice as I read the Scriptures. I listen as God's Spirit teaches me to discern truth from error, to "put things together," and to see them from his perspective.

Inner Impressions

I believe it is this shared perspective that results in the "inner impressions" many Christians take to be God's voice. Any time we get close to someone, we learn to intuitively understand his point of view. For example, when I set out to buy a present for a close friend, I search for a gift that will perfectly fit the person and the occasion. I search high and low, looking at innumerable options, but knowing immediately what won't do. Then suddenly I get a brainstorm and I know I have found the right gift. Sometimes this understanding seems to come out of thin air, so I say, "It just came to me." Such insights may seem miraculous, but generally they are not. If I am in regular communion with my friend, I am "listening" even when no words are exchanged. I "listen" to my friend's personality.

A Christian who is in constant communion with God and his Word will wake up to many such insights. If you are talking to God about your concerns, you will get promptings that seem to come from outside you. They may just flash into your mind: "Call Jane; she's lonely." "Stop what you're doing and pray, right now." It is good to pay close attention to such ideas, to consider seriously whether they come from the heart of God. They are not infallible instincts. They can be wrong, just as my instinct about the right present can be wrong. Sometimes a little skepticism is in order. The classic case comes when one believer announces to another believer that God has told him that she should marry him. Her answer should be, "Let God tell me too; he knows me."

These inner promptings are often right, however, and more often right as we grow to know God more. They should be listened to and responded to. Ignoring them because you are not a hundred percent sure they come from God is the wrong thing to do. At the very least, consult other friends who know God. If you are doubtful, ask God to repeat himself, to steer you right, to correct you or stop you if you have misread him and are headed in the wrong direction. He is actively engaged in this conversation.

A very important turning in my life came not long after I graduated from college. I got a job in a small publishing firm. I loved the work. I was getting lots of opportunities and my bosses promised more.

I had only been at the firm four or five months when a call came from another publisher whom I'd encountered in my job search. We met for lunch and he offered me a job. I told him I would think about the offer, but I was frank—I doubted I would want to switch jobs so soon. Out of politeness, because I respected him, I said I would let him know one way or the other by a certain date. I also said I would pray about it.

I did pray. But I really didn't think there was any way I would want to change. It didn't make sense to me when my current job was going so well.

The day came when I had promised to give a definite answer. I was quite prepared to say no and stay in my current job. I continued to pray, however, as I had been doing all along. I asked God to make it clear to me if I was going in the wrong direction. Then I went to bed. I would call the publisher in the morning.

I didn't sleep. For most of the night I lay awake, praying and thinking. By morning I had a very clear, strong sense that I should change jobs. And I felt very close to God.

God didn't address me by name or speak audibly. In the context of our relationship, though, I think he nudged me. I had asked for help. He gave it. I found myself seeing a new perspective and desiring new horizons. I changed my mind and did it in God's company.

Now I ask myself: Did I know subconsciously all along that I should change? Did my prayers just bring to the surface something in my feelings that I had been ignoring? Or did God really intervene?

My opinion is that he intervened, gently. On my own I would not have chosen to switch jobs no matter how much psychoanalysis I did. I can't prove that, however, not even to myself. All I know is that I was talking to God about what concerned me, and I was listening.

I am so glad I listened. The old job, it turned out, was headed for a dead end. Within six months I was very, very glad I had left. The new job was wonderful, a great chance to work with people who became my friends and mentors for life.

I believe in praying and I believe in listening to those inner promptings. By listening you are learning to walk in personal relationship with the God of the universe. As every person in a happy marriage will tell you, you have to learn to listen even to what is not said out loud. If you want communion with your spouse, you must learn to read her personality and respond. The same with God.

How Precious Are Words

My grandfather, a Presbyterian missionary, suffered a stroke in his old age and had global aphasia for the last ten years of his life. This strange ailment takes away the ability to communicate in words, whether written or spoken. Apparently the stroke scrambles the communication pathways of the brain. My grandfather could still think clearly, but he could not communicate his thoughts. His words came out garbled, as though he were speaking a foreign language. He could rarely understand our words either.

He had the stroke on a visit to Pakistan. After he had recovered enough to travel, he was put on a plane to England where my mother met him. One of his urgent wishes, which he communicated through gestures, was to go to a good Shakespearean theater. He thought that if he could hear someone speak in clear, stentorian tones he would understand. He was sadly disappointed.

The letters he wrote were extremely curious. They looked at first glance just like his normal hand, but a closer look revealed that the sentences were garbled. "I will need a little time to unravel this," I thought when I first tried to read one. When I tried, I found I could not make any sense of it at all.

An occasional word would come out of my grandfather's mouth indisputably right, but my grandfather never knew whether it was right or wrong. They all sounded right to him when he spoke. He maintained most of his memory of the Psalms, however, and his ability to lead in prayer. These circuits of the brain, I imagine, were so broad from frequent use that they were not destroyed with all the rest.

It was possible to communicate simple information to my grandfather through gestures, facial expressions, and tone of voice. This was tedious but it worked. We did not really need to communicate much. My grandfather was retired and his needs were cared for, so he really had little information he needed to exchange. Still, for all of us who loved him, those ten years were agony. He lived with people he loved, but he could not speak or understand. He was lonely. His communion with others had been broken abruptly and terribly. Words had been taken away.

He would come to Thanksgiving dinner at my parents' house, his broad Scots face beaming, to hold babies on his knee and enjoy a good meal with a family that adored him. He would try to talk, to crack a good joke as in the old days, or to describe the questions he had about why God allowed him to suffer. We could understand that he was trying to joke or make theological conversation about suffering. But we could not get the joke or follow his line of thought. We would try, flounder, fail, smile, and shake our heads apologetically. Eventually my grandfather would find a comfortable chair in the corner and doze. He let us know that he wanted to die.

Conversation is a gift. Our words back and forth are crucial to personal relationships, not because they communicate information but because they bind us together. Lose this gift through a stroke or Alzheimer's and you will learn the deep sadness of being alone, really alone.

I take this as a terrible and penetrating challenge to speak my words to God as often as I talk to myself. I think Paul meant just this when he urged people to "pray continually" (1 Thessalonians 5:17). It is also a challenge to read God's Word and hear him speaking personally through the voice of the Holy Spirit. When we do this, his personality and his plans become imbedded in our minds so that he can speak to us through them as often as we speak to him. Is the communication perfect? Is it all that we could wish? No.

But it is valuable nonetheless. It makes all the difference between being alone in the universe and having a personal relationship with its Creator.

The Words of the Last Day

Many people dream of the questions they will ask when they finally see Jesus face-to-face. They expect to clear up all the issues they have wondered about. But when the Bible lifts the curtain drawn over the age to come, that is not what we hear. The book of Revelation gives us a picture of what to expect, and it is far from the graduate-level seminar we need to satisfy our doubts and wonderings. We are promised no long chats, no questions-and-answers about the meaning of suffering. The only words mentioned are songs of praise: "To him who sits on the throne and to the Lamb be praise and honor and glory and power, for ever and ever!" (Revelation 5:13)

What does God say to us? According to the picture Jesus drew in Matthew 25, his words to us will be an invitation: "Come, you who are blessed by my Father; take your inheritance, the kingdom prepared for you since the creation of the world" (Matthew 25:34).

I imagine an antiphony that will go on forever. "Praise and honor and glory and power," we will sing, while he says again and again, "Come! Come in!"

Here is an interesting fact: these words—praise and invitation—are what our life of conversation with God consists of already. When we speak to God we begin and end with praise, as Jesus taught us to do in his Lord's Prayer. And God's word to us in the Bible is one extended invitation, urging us to come in and join him. Perhaps, then, that final, most personal confrontation with God will seem strangely familiar—much like the way we have been conversing with him all along, only more so. Much, much more so.

5

Meet the Family

So you have talked, hour after hour of intimate conversation. You feel quite sure that this is the relationship you hoped for. You are getting to know each other.

But no relationship grows in a vacuum. You have to meet the family.

I think back to when I fell in love with Popie. I could have spent any amount of time with her, getting closer. I was less enthusiastic about spending time with her family. Not that I disliked them. But I had chosen Popie, and her family came as an unsought extra.

Popie's family lived in the South; my family were northerners. Her father was a doctor, mine a pastor. Her mother wept while telling me that Popie had chosen not to rush a sorority in college; I decided not to mention that my mother had helped ban sororities at her school.

I wasn't entirely comfortable negotiating such differences. On a practical level there was no reason I had to. Both Popie and I lived thousands of miles away from her parents' home. We were both several years out of school, financially independent, and well launched into our working lives. We could have established our relationship without bothering about our families, as some people do.

We never considered that for a moment, though. We both knew that a relationship cut off from family would be brittle, superficial, and isolated.

Our families carry so much of who we are. Popie's parents had raised her; her brothers and sister had grown up with her. They held long memories of her, thousands upon thousands of hours of her life at every stage from infancy on. And they had rubbed off on her. The books they read and TV shows they watched were part of her world. Their senses of humor tickled hers. The house where she had grown up, where every corner and every stair held her memories, was their house. Not only did they know her old stories, in most cases they *were* her old stories. They knew her high school friends and her grade school friends. They were the people she loved and the people she reacted against.

Ghost Images

Sometimes artists rework a canvas, painting over their earlier ideas as they refine their work. Centuries later, art curators use X-rays and other technical apparatus to "see" under the paint. The earlier figures may appear, "ghosts" that reveal a shadow history of the painting. Our families are a little like that—ghosts that shadow us wherever we go. You can't see my family when you meet me, but they are there.

Years ago I picked up an envelope, glanced at it, and discovered something a little frightening. The return address, which I had written myself, was in my father's handwriting. I had certainly never tried to imitate his hand, but without any intention my writing had come to approximate his. He was with me, guiding my hand, though no one could see him.

Another eerie experience came while writing a book, *Knowing the Face of God*. It was more personal than anything I had written, and I was extremely focused on doing my very best work. As I wrote, I felt dueling aspects of my personality emerge—and they were the personalities of my parents. I felt my dad's quick, intuitive leaps. I felt my mom's steady piety. I knew both those characters intimately, since they had raised me, and I discovered that their voices now spoke through my words.

Many people have an experience something like that while raising children. Talking to them or scolding them, parents hear words they remember their own parents saying. They may have vowed never to say such things, but the words just come out—as though their parents were speaking through them.

For all these reasons, when you fall in love and go to "meet the parents," you really go to meet your prospective spouse. You will not only spend Christmas and Thanksgiving with your in-laws. You will spend every day with them, as your wife reacts to you in the way her mother reacted to her father, or as your husband sits in front of the TV just as his father did. They say you should check out your in-laws to see how your spouse will look in thirty years. Truthfully, you don't have to wait that long.

Our families are part of who we are—even if we don't like them, even if we don't visit them, even if we have set out to be their opposite. If you want to form a strong personal relationship with someone, you need to know the family.

God Is the Root of Everything

Does this apply to God? In one sense you cannot know God's family the way I sought to know Popie's. God doesn't "take after" anybody. "He was with God in the beginning," John says of Jesus, and "through him all things were made" (John 1:3). Popie has roots, but Jesus *is* the root—of everything.

Meet the Family

Yet God does have family—those who "take after" him. Knowing God through his family is not so much like my going to meet Popie's parents. It is more like meeting our children. If you want to really "get" Popie in depth, you need to know Katie, Chase, and Silas, our adult children. Popie has rubbed off on them, and they are "like her."

God has offspring too. The human race is "like God," for he made us all "in his image." However much that image gets distorted, it still can be seen.

Practically speaking, though, not all God's offspring have been in close relation to him. God's image may be imprinted on our genetic heritage, but it only fully develops through his personal influence. The Bible spotlights God's family in the church. All humanity is meant to be included in God's family, but the ones who carry on the relationship and show the effects of God's personality day by day are church people.

This can be hard to believe. In church you typically find paunchy middle-aged guys talking about their golf game, elderly ladies with blue hair, young parents so locked into family life they barely know the world exists outside of Under-12 soccer. How would you ever find God here? Where in the swirl of Sunday clothes, un-hip music, and a ritual involving nibbles of cracker and sips of wine would you find the Maker of heaven and earth? How exactly would you hear his voice in the preacher who starts every sermon with a slightly stale joke? Will you meet God in the coffee hour while eating a donut? Will he turn up at the youth group, in the face of the teenage kid who can't stop poking his girlfriend to make her giggle? I want to know a heavenly God who is truly extraordinary, and the family of Jesus is an extremely ordinary group. Practically speaking, how do I find God here?

These are hard questions. And yet I will stick with this assertion: to know God, you have to know his family. Just as my relationship to Popie would be brittle and narrow if I tried to cut out her family, so relating to God without his church family would take away the breadth and warmth, the humanity, of relating to him. For in the church the character of God takes on human shape. Jesus rubs off on these people.

The Place to Find God?

Church may be an odd place to look for God, but people do still go there to find him. Suppose one of your neighbors or coworkers feels a heavenly longing —the "desire which no experience in this world can satisfy" that C. S. Lewis wrote of. Chances are that he or she will turn up in church.

Meet the Family

Why church? Well, where else? The one thing most people know about churches is that they claim to be God places.

If you go to church looking and hoping to find God, you may well begin a relationship with him there. Somebody may tell you that you can ask God into your heart, and you may respond by doing so. Church — plain, ordinary church — is the most likely place for this mind-crashing event to take place, the God of heaven forming a lasting relationship with a regular human.

If you begin a relationship with Jesus in church, it is also there, strangely enough, that you will probably absorb Jesus' character. If you ask a new believer to describe Jesus, he probably can't say much more than "loving" or "merciful." If you ask him to describe Jesus' family members whom he has met in church, a lot more information is immediately accessible.

He knows that these people are friendly, that they care for him, and that they seem to know Jesus. He listens carefully for what they say, and he is drawn into the way of life that they are following.

Typically, a lot of trivial behavior gets imitated. Do the church people all have a black leather-bound *NIV Student Bible*? The new believer buys the same Bible, right down to the black leather cover. Do they punctuate their prayers with odd phrases such as "we just magnify you, Lord"? So does the new believer. Do the church members abstain from drinking? He quits drinking himself. Do they wear sweaters and slacks to church? So does he. To him, following Jesus means living like Jesus' family—even dressing like Jesus' family.

This family, like most families, is a mixture of good and bad. It has taken some of its identity from Jesus, but a lot of it comes from other less desirable sources. Nevertheless, among these people the new believer finds human beings who have been shaped by Jesus' personality. Through them, Jesus rubs off on him—and so do a lot of other cultural influences.

Cultural Entrapment

At one time this cultural entrapment worried me. I supposed my ideal Christian was a philosopher who would choose to believe in Jesus after careful research into all the world's religions and philosophies. His or her faith would spring straight from the New Testament, with no other influences involved.

I have changed my mind. Few such philosopher-Christians exist, and those that do often turn out to be lonely and unstable in their relationship with God. They just have nowhere to call home.

By contrast, people enmeshed in the life of a Christian community usually grow in faith—and they tend to stick. The reason for this vitality is obvious. You can learn more about a man—in this case, Jesus—by spending an hour with his family than you can by almost any other method, apart from spending time with the man himself. In the church new believers soak up a real working sense of how Jesus rubs off on people. That is why missionaries work so hard to start a church when they go to pioneer territory. Jesus may remain an abstraction, a "god," until people experience him within the life of his family.

I find this true to my own experience. The churches I grew up in were very ordinary. Many of their cultural assumptions had nothing to do with Jesus. But in those churches I grew up knowing people who showed me what the doctrines of Christianity actually looked like in human life. It wasn't abstract; it wasn't philosophical. It was human.

I think of my high school youth group sponsor, Bud Oslin. Bud was no Bible scholar and no theologian. He was a loud, funny, outgoing character who talked to me and made me feel valuable. I was an adolescent riding a storm of anxiety and self-doubt. For me, Bud was an embodiment of grace. He made me understand something of what Jesus was really like, in flesh and blood.

I realize I might have found characters like Bud elsewhere—leading Boy Scouts or coaching YMCA basketball. When you meet them in church, though, there is a very close association with Jesus. You read about Jesus in the Bible and hear lessons about him in church, and you get to know people who love Jesus and live grace-filled lives. So you begin to put it all together, to understand more about Jesus as a person as you spend time with his family.

An Ongoing Family Life

It is no good loving family in some generic sense. You have to settle down and appreciate a certain group of people in a certain place. Like all families, God's family is down-to-earth and local.

If you are not involved in a church, you have to find one, get involved, and get to know the family you find there. If you already belong to a church, you have to learn how to put energy and interest into the relationships.

Sometimes it means working through issues. A person who has never forgiven his family for their failings can never be fully at peace with himself. Similarly, a Christian must learn to love and appreciate those who are family, regardless of their faults. Recognizing, even rebelling against, the limitations of your home church is natural. But real maturity comes when you accept those limitations and see beyond them to the fundamental character of Jesus.

This appreciation may cost great inner turmoil. Many people spend years in therapy working through their relationships to family; likewise, many Christians feel wounded by their church family. Sometimes they need the help of a counselor or a spiritual director to come to terms with their experiences in church.

As people grow, they learn to differentiate between Jesus' influence on the church and the other influences of culture and circumstances. In my relationship to Popie's family, I learned certain peculiarities of each member. But those aren't Popie's peculiarities; they are her family's. I can tell the difference rather easily. Similarly, though I grew up Presbyterian, I can tell the difference between Jesus and the Presbyterian fondness for committee meetings, between Jesus and my Protestant heritage of individualism, between Jesus and my American church assumptions that large numbers are always a good thing.

Such discernment becomes extremely difficult when abusive people gain influence in church. When young Christians get abused—sexually, emotionally, or spiritually—it scars their memories, and they have a very difficult time separating the abuse from Jesus. Jesus' family, if they allow such abuse, can turn the young and the tender off Jesus for life. No wonder that Jesus warned so sternly against those who abuse little ones by causing them to sin (Matthew 18:6).

The Extended Family

As time goes by, you begin to see that there's a bigger, more extended family to learn from. Popie's family has several branches—in Alabama, in Mississippi, and in Tennessee. As the years have passed, I've become more familiar with them, and I've seen a richness and breadth in the family that I couldn't see in her immediate family of origin. I get a better feeling for the big picture of her life by seeing all the cousins, aunts, and uncles splayed out across the landscape of the South.

Sometimes the extended family has a slightly different take on the family stories. For example, Popie's dad grew up in rural Alabama. The first stories I heard of his childhood emphasized poverty: he sometimes walked barefoot to school and he got just one small present for Christmas. He told me the saddest Christmas story I ever heard. One Christmas his only present was a top. He excitedly wound it up and spun it—right into the fireplace. The top, made of lead, melted to a puddle.

Meeting his cousins, I heard a different version of his childhood. "Henry always had money." I learned that he grew up living part-time with his grandparents, who were poor dirt farmers during the Depression, and part-time with his father, who had a steady job as a mail carrier. His childhood poverty was real, but it was a complex reality that I could best understand by meeting the larger family.

We understand Jesus better as we get to know other branches of *his* family thriving all over the world. People from different cultures and situations get to know different aspects of Jesus. For example, those who live where witchcraft and spirit possession are vital realities may grasp a dimension of Jesus' power over evil that I don't easily get. Those who live in poverty may understand Jesus' concern for the poor in a way that rich Western Christians don't. The more we appreciate such people and their perspectives, the more we will see Jesus clearly in all his splendor. Some of the greatest joys of my life in Jesus have come through knowing his extended family around the world.

And don't forget those family members who are no longer living. For two thousand years Jesus has befriended people. Some have written down their thoughts. I have learned a great deal about Jesus from Augustine, who died 1,600 years ago.

Even Christians who didn't write left a record in the traditions of the church. I realize that evangelical Protestants like me have taken little interest in tradition.

We have tended to see it as getting in the way of seeing Jesus rather than helping. Indeed, tradition can block the view. But most traditions began with people who loved Jesus and learned to relate to him in a certain way. Not all of these traditions reflect Jesus, but they do all reflect Jesus' family—and through them, you can sense some of Jesus' input. (So-called nontraditional churches also have their traditions, as you will discover if you propose changing anything.)

My background made me think of Jesus as someone particularly interested in my mind—my beliefs and my attitudes. That is an important tradition, because Jesus is indeed concerned for the mind that he created. My tradition, however, downplayed the importance of my physical body and my physical surroundings. I didn't think Jesus saw much significance in these.

When I lived in France and prayed each week in a Gothic cathedral, though, I developed a different perspective on Jesus. The cathedral's incredible beauty became familiar to me as a place for prayer. I began to glimpse the reason why so much wealth and work had gone into church buildings. Some of Jesus' family clearly cared about physical surroundings. Perhaps he did too. I began to see Jesus as one who appreciates worship in stone and glass as well as thought and attitude. It expanded my mind on Jesus.

When the Bible refers to the church as "Christ's body," it means that he lives in and through his followers. Watch these people, and you will gain a greater feeling for Jesus. When you see them, you see him.

Family Meals

One more thing. In my experience, you get to know a family over meals. Whether at the daily supper table, the annual Thanksgiving feast, or the wedding banquet, when you break bread together you grow closer. Meals are essential to relationship.

I don't believe I have ever had a personal relationship in which no food or drink were shared. A relationship can go only so far before somebody says, "Let's go get a cup of coffee." Sometimes the amount consumed is so small as to be symbolic: a sip of champagne after a toast, for example. In some cultures, you drink a glass of water or a cup of tea when you visit the home—nothing more. Always, though, you share some food or drink together.

If you want to know Jesus by knowing his family, you must eat and drink with them. That is exactly what Jesus told his followers to do when he took them upstairs just before his death and introduced a meal modeled from the Jewish Passover family meal.

We don't always think of it as a meal. Communion, or the Lord's Supper, or the Eucharist, as it is variously known, has become an austere, gravely hushed ceremony. Its chief and most obvious characteristic—that the bread and wine are food—has been buried under centuries of solemn religious observance. Yet Jesus inaugurated the Lord's Supper as part of a meal. That you eat only a token amount does not matter. You are joining the family of Jesus for a bite.

Jesus told his followers to eat the meal as a way of remembering him. Some people think memory is a library of facts stored in a remote corner of the brain. From that perspective, a meal in memory of Jesus seems to consign him to a place as dry as dust. That may be why some churches don't celebrate the Lord's Supper very often. They want to celebrate a living Jesus, not "remember" him!

Augustine described a mental experiment that routed this view of memory. He simply attempted to define life in the present.

Is living in the present "one day at a time," Augustine asked? No, because right now the morning is in the past and the evening is in the future. Is the present perhaps a very short time? A minute, for instance? No, for a minute breaks into seconds, and half of the seconds are past and half yet to come. The harder you try to define the present, the narrower the present becomes. It is like a sharply honed blade on the front edge of memory, cutting through the future and turning it to the past. The present has such a fleeting existence that no meaning can survive in it. Even a single word has no meaning. By the time we pronounce the second syllable, the first syllable is in the past, in our memory. Thus if we could only listen in the present, we would never understand a word. We would only be bombarded with fragments of sound.

The same is true of meeting people. If we live in the present alone, they are constant strangers to us. We cannot understand their words; we cannot make sense of their faces. Without memory, a "personality" does not exist for us, and a "person" is unknown to us—only a leering face, making noise.

So when we eat and drink with other children of Jesus, remembering his death and resurrection, we are doing just what we must do to experience Jesus as a living person. Do you think the disciples ever forgot that last meal with him, the event that propelled him into his great sacrifice? Neither should we. We are invited to share in that last meal and to share in the memories. Without memory, held in common by his family, he would be merely a bright light, a strange face—even if he appeared visibly before us in unspeakable glory. Memory enables his presence to have personality.

Jesus invited us to this meal. He is the host. We don't see him or hear him; we see his family members. Their lives, shaped by his, show us his personality fleshed out in humanity. Their memories, shared together, help us put together the whole person of Jesus. We deepen in our relationship to him as we share a meal with his family members.

6

Suffering Together

Both my parents died in the past year—my mother in October after a short, sudden illness, and my father four months later, after ten years of Alzheimer's. Both deaths were peaceful. My parents had lived admirable lives, and they passed away surrounded by children who adored them.

Even so-called "good deaths" involve suffering, though. I found nothing easy about watching either of them struggle for their last breath. Yet there was one good result: I feel closer to siblings and in-laws who shared the experience with me. We spent many hours together, watching and caring.

When we are together now I feel slightly raw, as though I have lost skin and am tender to the touch. We are bound together in a way I have not felt before. I think our relationships are permanently changed.

Suffering does that to us. The people we grow closest to are often those who share it with us.

We have all experienced, I daresay, opening up with a friend about some deep problem we face and finding afterward that we feel much closer to that friend. It happens all the time in medical support groups. People don't even know each other in the beginning, and they may have little in common. As they open up about fear and pain and the drudgery of medical treatment, however, they often find themselves launched into extraordinary fellowship.

What Are We Looking For?

I don't know why God permits suffering, but I do know that suffering exists, no matter what I think of it. Even in a society trying to abolish suffering, people will continue to suffer. And sometimes, clearly, that suffering draws them deeper into relationships with others.

Suffering strips away everything that is not central to life—ambition, vanity, love of money. All your great plans seem remote when you suffer. What matters is the reality you face that minute.

You lose your sense of being in charge. If you could eliminate the suffering you would, but you cannot. You are not God. You cannot order life around.

And so you turn to other people to share your emptiness. Sometimes you do so silently—misery is simply written on your face. More often you use words, telling someone what you are going through. And if someone receives what you say, simply listening compassionately, what a wonderful gift. "Here at last is somebody I can share this with," you may think.

In the face of real suffering, you lose the self-consciousness, competitiveness, flippancy, and pride that keep people apart. When these barriers to the soul are down, deep relationships become possible.

Jesus as the Sufferer

But we are not talking about how to make friends with other people; we are talking about God. Can you have a personal relationship with him through suffering?

More than any other person in history, more than anyone you have ever known, Jesus suffered. Suffering is central to his identity. The biographical sketches known as the Gospels tell about his suffering and death more than any other topic. The emblem of his life to this day is a Roman torture machine, the cross.

He suffered incredible physical pain. Execution by crucifixion is roughly the same as having hooks rammed through your hands and feet and being strung up in the sun until you die. Every move you make—even breathing—tears at your wounds. Gravity puts all your weight on the gashes where the nails have cut holes in your extremities. Romans used crucifixion for the horror, to warn would-be rebels. It was an awful way to die.

Jesus' suffering was undeserved. He was innocent—entirely, blessedly innocent. He never hurt anybody. A close friend betrayed him. His own people turned him over to their worst enemies. Then his followers ran away and left him without a word of support at his trial. Everything about his execution was built on lies and deliberate distortions of his record. He was utterly alone at the end.

He suffered in public. His struggle was not carried out in a bedroom at home or in a hospital room behind a curtain, but instead beside the highway, with idlers jeering and passersby staring. Another man being executed yelled insults, thinking Jesus contemptible. Jesus had set out to change the world, to lead his people into a life that would draw the whole world to God. At his death, he appeared an utter failure, publicly disgraced. There are only so many ways a person can suffer, and Jesus suffered them all: physically, spiritually, and emotionally.

Therefore, if anyone understands your pain, Jesus does. In the hospital corridor, at the drug rehab check-in desk, at the morgue, at the family reunion where everybody turns against you, in the meeting in which your boss lays you off—wherever your worst nightmare of suffering occurs—Jesus is waiting to talk to you. He knows.

If you don't know Jesus as a sufferer, you don't know him in full. In the reality of his suffering lies a great opportunity to know him in the most intimate way.

Nobody Wants This Job

Nobody wants to suffer. If you are a healthy human being, every fiber in your body fights against it. You want it to stop, and you may complain bitterly to God, "Why me? Why are you doing this to me?"

That question gets asked quite often in the Bible. The Psalms, the Bible's hymnbook, voice bitter complaints. *Where are you, God?* the psalmists demand. *Why have you deserted me?* It sounds as though for them suffering led to the opposite of a good relationship with God.

Job was the ultimate case of angry suffering as he searched for a reason and demanded an answer from God. As the Old Testament book presents his case, he is caught in the ultimate injustice, suffering terrible pain not because he was bad but because he was good.

Job scorched heaven with his call for an explanation. He would not shrug his shoulders and quit asking. He kept demanding an answer from God, and at the end of the book he got it. God answered Job's questions with more questions—withering questions. "Where were you when I laid the earth's foundation?" Yahweh roared. "Tell me, if you understand. Who marked off its dimensions? Surely you know!" (Job 38:4–5) God gave Job, in a poetically grand manner, one instruction: Take the first three chapters of Genesis seriously. Do you understand that I made the heavens and the earth?

That argument is like Paul's in Romans 9: "How can a pot question the potter's methods?" It is almost impossible to think *up* in the order of creation—to understand the Creator from the position of the created. Think *down* to your created works, such as pots, the Bible says, and you may have some idea how crude your questions sound to God. The problem is not that man is so low but that God is so high—as high above us as we are above pots. The Creator cannot be a peer called into question by his creation.

Yet God's answer to Job has two sides. God told Job to shut up, but he did it by rewarding Job's noise—for God delivered the answer personally. God cared enough to come before Job's eyes. He would not—or could not—answer Job's questions the way Job wanted them answered, but he cared enough to come. Job got what every suffering believer longs for: the actual presence of God. And that was enough to satisfy him.

The Fellow-Sufferer

When you turn from the Old Testament to the New, you enter a very different environment. The New Testament writers never ask questions the way Job (or the psalmists or the prophets) did. They had seen God in the face of Jesus, and that changed everything. They had seen that God himself suffers.

So rather than carrying forward Job's questions, they carried on God's answer: We can meet God in our suffering, if we don't give up. "Be patient, then, brothers, until the Lord's coming. See how the farmer waits for the land to yield its valuable crop and how patient he is for the autumn and spring rains. You too, be patient and stand firm, because the Lord's coming is near" (James 5:7–8).

Unlike Job, the early Christians accepted suffering as normal. They lived with official and unofficial harassment, arrest, imprisonment, torture, and execution. They talked about it as a joy and a privilege, for Jesus was a fellow-sufferer. In suffering, they came into fellowship with Jesus in a deeply personal way. They wanted to be as near him and as like him as possible, to experience "the fellowship of sharing in his suffer-ings" (Philippians 3:10).

Where Cancer Fits

You might ask, "What does this have to do with me? Those people in the New Testament, with their posi-tive attitude toward suffering, were persecuted for their *faith*. I have no idea why I am suffering. It just seems pointless."

It's hard to say, "I'm suffering for my Lord," if you have the same problem your unbelieving neighbor has. Nothing marks cancer or divorce or a child on drugs as sacred.

The point, however, isn't that you accomplish great, sacred things for Jesus when you suffer. The point is that you draw closer to him, that you get to know him better.

Peter's first letter speaks of slaves suffering "in Jesus' steps" at the hands of brutal masters. They weren't beaten because of their faith. Slaves just get beaten. Peter tells them, "It is commendable if a man bears up under the pain of unjust suffering *because he is conscious of God....* To this you were called, because Christ suffered for you, leaving you an example, that you should follow in his steps" (1 Peter 2:19, 21, em-phasis added).

What makes their suffering valuable is their con-sciousness of God, who suffered. You can be conscious of God if you get beaten up for no reason. You can be conscious of God if cancer spreads through your body for no reason. You can be conscious of God if you're jobless at the age of fifty-eight. You can be conscious of God if somebody you love betrays you. In anything you suffer, you should know: Jesus has been there be-fore you. You can talk to him with confidence that he understands. It is all right to complain bitterly, for Jesus himself called out, "My God, my God, why have you forsaken me?" (Psalm 22:1).

Complete Honesty

In fact, if you want to come closer to Jesus, to deepen your personal relationship through suffering, speak to him with absolute emotional honesty. The more you open up, the more potential for you to grasp his fellowship.

One way is to pray the Psalms. They are beautifully expressive, with the full range of joy and pain. If you are so angry you can't pray, let the Psalms give you a voice. They gave Jesus words when he was suffering on the cross, for he quoted from them when he cried out.

Most people start with an image of God as the per-fect, all-powerful, up-in-heaven God—one who has

never had a problem. The real face of God is Jesus'
face, Jesus suffering and dying because he has been
betrayed. You can talk to that kind of God.

If you pay attention in almost any church you'll
get reminders of who you are relating to. You'll see a
cross displayed; think about what it means for Jesus. In
the weeks leading up to Easter, many churches focus
especially on all that happened to Jesus on the way
to his death. He suffered unbearably. Now suffering is
something he shares with you.

No relationship can be very deep that does not
include a dose of shared anguish. With Jesus you have
more than a dose. The Bible greatly emphasizes his
suffering. One reason that emphasis is made, surely, is
that the writers believed in a personal relationship with
God—and they understood the suffering Jesus as the
only God we could relate to.

7

Sharing Work

"What do you do?"

It is the most common conversation starter—the easiest place to go after exchanging names. We don't ask, "What are your strengths and weaknesses?" or "What do you value most in life?" Instead we ask, "What do you do?" Anybody can answer this question, and the response is usually factual: "I'm a student" or "I write software" or "I'm a plumber."

The information is helpful in getting to know someone, for a major piece of life is filled in. You can ask other questions—"Where did you grow up?" "Where did you go to school?" "What's your all-time favorite movie?"—but "What do you do?" is more basic.

Your work touches who you are. A teacher is different from a dentist or a welder. And if you're ashamed of your job, or you hate it, that also tells a lot about your life.

Even people who love their work find some aspects painful. For me, pain often comes with editors. I know I need their objective judgment. Even after all these years of accepting criticism, though, it cuts. It's like going to the dentist for drilling. You lay yourself down in the chair and wait for the nasty whining sting to begin penetrating your teeth. Is there a writer who hasn't wanted to quit a hundred times? And yet I love my work passionately.

If you want to know me, you have to know that I am a writer. If you want to know me deeply, you have to penetrate both the joy and pain I feel in my work. In much the same way, you have to penetrate the joy and pain a stay-at-home mom feels, or that of a contractor or a nurse. Our work is linked to our identity.

Some people, it is true, live for what they do after work. I coached Little League for many years, and some of the men I coached with fit that description. They got through the day in order to follow their true vocation, which was teaching little boys an arcane and complicated game. In that case, you had to know them in Little League to know them fully, just as you would have to investigate model trains or chess or quilting to get to the heart of other people. Some people find their true work-of-the-heart in cooking for the homeless shelter or in leading Bible studies or in working on political campaigns. If you want a deepening personal relationship with such people you have to learn about their passion. They may not do it for a living, but for them it is the true answer to the question, "What do you do?"

Praying about Work

I reckon work to be the third-leading category of prayer requests, after health and family. People beg God for jobs, for success in business endeavors, for wisdom about career choices, and for better relations with bosses and coworkers. They bring extremely personal worries about work to God because they want to make a real connection with him. (Of course, they also want help.) Work is an important part of who they are, so they talk about it to God.

Strikingly, we rarely turn that around. We rarely talk to God about *his* work.

"Hello, God, what do you do?"

It is a good question to ask. Certainly it is a question God seems eager to answer. A very large proportion of the Bible addresses what God has done, is doing, and wants to do. You might call the Bible his professional resume.

The first words in the Bible introduce God as a worker. "In the beginning God created ..." It goes on with obvious relish to tell how he made everything in the world. Genesis generates a lot of debate about the process of creation—for example, how long it took. But there has never been any doubt that Genesis describes God's creative activity—his work.

If you know God's work, you know a lot about God. I remember walking through a park one spring with a man who pointed out the contrast between a small, dribbling fountain in the center of the park and the tall flowering trees all around. "Human beings measure out goods by the cup," my friend said, referring to the fountain, "while God flings beauty extravagantly," referring to the trees. It was a new thought to me, to look at the natural world as the craftsmanship of God and a sign of his character.

Some doubter might bring up other examples of nature: spiders that eat their mates or parasites that destroy their host. But even in such cases, the immense inventiveness of God's world pays testament to his creativity. Not all his paintings are bright and cheery, but all teem with life and brilliance.

Science, then, explores God's work world. He has put his heart into these marvels of nature. Do you think it is an accident that birds can fly?

God's work in the natural world is not just marvelous, it is beautiful. I sometimes like to imagine that nobody had ever seen a tree until one day an explorer to distant lands found one and transported it to New York. He put the tree on display in the Museum of Modern Art. Artists from everywhere began to gather, to stand in awe. That one tree would put all other art to shame—so beautiful, so intricate, so simple, with such subtleties of texture and color. Look at how it catches the slightest wind! Would you not like to know the artist? Doesn't appreciating the tree help you understand the character of the artist?

But a tree is far from the summit of God's creativity. His genius is seen most of all in human beings—in you and me. What amazing, complex creatures we are. Here are animals who decode their own genome, make movies, invent ways to fly although they lack wings and to swim under the ocean although they lack gills. They write wonderful novels and paint fascinating pictures. They invent computers to make fabulous calculations and then play games on them. The range of human emotion and thought and invention is, well, godlike. After all, God made us and we should marvel at him every day. We should learn to make the connection: the complexity of humans reflects the astonishing creativity of the mind of God.

God Sweats Blood

God's work also brings him pain. I know of a man who built a highly successful business. When he was near retirement age his own son organized a coup, stripped him of corporate control, and managed not just to drive him out but to wreck the company.

So it is with God. His best and most beautiful project has turned against him, has turned against itself and against the rest of God's beautiful work. God's children spit at him, practice genocide on each other, and pollute the environment. We have wiped out entire species, hardly noticing or caring.

Yet God is not daunted. God's ongoing work reaches its climax in response to humanity's most despicable destruction. The Bible tells the story of how God chose Abraham to redeem a family of nomads, how he schooled that family in Egypt and in their great escape from slavery, how he used them to build a tiny kingdom at a crossroads of the world and protected them from the collisions of empires. How he worked to teach them how to live with love for him and for each other, how he chastised them and pursued them with love songs and threats. How he sent his Son to regather them, how that Son was betrayed and murdered and how, in the strangest reversal, that betrayal and death turned into a miracle of life and resurrection not just for God's chosen people but for the whole world.

God is the dramatist in this great play. God is also the actor. He sweat blood over this production. It is a work full of pain and pathos, fully capturing the ironic horrors of life. It *is* life. He put his life into it; he would die for it. What a piece of work!

The better you know God's work, the more you talk to him about it and admire him for it, the better you will know him. He will stop being a cardboard cutout of "God," but will be, to you, a fully rounded figure. Part of nurturing a deep personal relationship with God is appreciating his work.

Joining In

A man who graduated from MIT in the early 1940s told me a story about his senior year, when all graduating students were mysteriously called in to hear a presentation from a possible employer. They only half listened to this recruiter, for most of them had already made plans to join other firms. The recruiter's conclusion, however, caught their full attention: "I hope you are attracted to the opportunities I have presented," he said, "because I can personally guarantee that every one of you will join my company." He represented the top-secret Manhattan Project, which used the military draft to enlist MIT's entire senior class.

Not everyone who worked for the Manhattan Project knew what it was about. Most people knew only the narrow work of their own division. Security was so tight that even spouses could not be told anything. The man who told me this story said that throughout the war his wife had no idea what he did. Then one morning before going to work, he told her, "Be sure to listen to the radio today. I think you'll find out what I've been doing all this time." It was the day the atomic bomb was dropped on Hiroshima.

That day his wife understood his work. At the same time she got insight into the work of the human race—a frightening look into our potential for harm, the work of our best and most inventive minds.

Everything was secret in the Manhattan Project, and then came sudden revelation. There is a note something like this when God's work is described in the New Testament: "Concerning this salvation, the prophets, who spoke of the grace that was to come to you, searched intently and with the greatest care, trying to find out the time and circumstances to which the Spirit of Christ in them was pointing when he predicted the sufferings of Christ and the glories that would follow.... Even angels long to look into these things" (1 Peter 1:10–12).

God's work became as suddenly clear as the Manhattan Project did on the day of Hiroshima. But God's revelation had just the opposite significance: it was entirely happy news. God is a lover and a peacemaker and a life-giver—and his work in the death and resurrection of Jesus shows it.

The apostle Paul was one of those who could not stop staring and marveling at this explosion of understanding. "Surely you have heard about the administration of God's grace that was given to me for you, that is, the mystery made known to me by revelation, as I have already written briefly.... The mystery of Christ ... was not made known to men in other generations as it has now been revealed.... This mystery is that through the gospel the Gentiles are heirs together with Israel, members together of one body, and sharers together in the promise in Christ Jesus" (Ephesians 3:2–6).

You cannot read this without feeling Paul's tremendous excitement. After centuries of obscurity, God's plan to undo all the division and hatred between peoples and races had come into the clear. For the first time, Paul could see what God was doing. And through understanding God's work—and joining in that work—Paul could know God.

Joining in? Yes, Paul was not an ivory-tower theologian who merely wanted to sit back and admire God's plan. He understood that he had been invited to participate in the work, to labor side by side with God in the reshaping of the world. So have you.

Working Side by Side

The person I have worked with most closely over many years is a fellow writer and editor, Philip Yancey. We are temperamentally just about as unlike as two people can be. But we know each other deeply because we have worked so closely together.

Whether you are digging holes for fence posts or organizing a corporate buyout, the back and forth of teamwork opens up the possibilities of knowing each other closer than a brother—of understanding how each other thinks, of learning to anticipate each other's moves. When Philip and I talk about our work, we use a kind of shorthand. We know what the other will say almost before he speaks.

God invites us into a *working* relationship. It has been so all along. God did not introduce himself to Moses in order to start a theological discussion. He recruited Moses to lead his people against Pharaoh and through the desert. It was difficult, scary work—and to do it God initiated a personal relationship with Moses, a partnership.

Sharing Work

When Jesus called his disciples, he was not inviting them to go camping. He started a movement. He recruited and trained leaders to accomplish his goals. They became a team, bonded together to carry on the work after Jesus had gone. He promised to keep working with them and helping them through his Spirit.

That promise extends to you. He has invited you into a personal relationship, but the context is work. Not that he expects you to blaze any trails. He has done all the really hard work. He has led the way, and now you—and all of us together—are meant to walk in his steps. That means paying close attention to the kind of ministry he did and then carrying it on. In that context you can and will deepen in your personal relationship to God—working together. He promises to work with you through his Spirit, from the first day to the last.

Nor is the work a matter of just you and Jesus, alone against the world. He recruited twelve disciples and they worked as a team. Whenever he sent them out on special missions, they went with at least one companion. The twelve were the start of a movement, and what we call the church is the continuation of that movement. It involves a large number of individuals working together for the same purpose. There is no question of individual brilliance. Jesus has group work in mind.

The Family Business

This is a family business. In the church, God's children work together. We get to know each other very well as we work together, and we get to know God, the Father of the family, who heads the work.

The Bible gives us lots of instructions about the work, beginning with, "Love the Lord your God with all your heart and with all your soul and with all your mind, . . . and love your neighbor as yourself" (Matthew 22:37 – 39). There is also Jesus' Great Commission to "make disciples of all nations, baptizing them . . . and teaching them to obey everything I have commanded you" (Matthew 28:19).

But you don't need to worry about doing great feats by yourself. Nor is it necessarily your job to figure out a plan of work for taking the Gospel to the whole world. In a family business, you do what the family needs you to do. Go to church, get to know the family, and find out what you can do in the family business. I have yet to see a church that does not have extra work waiting for the workers. Just get there and take your assignment. Once you're involved and engaged, you can work with others to figure out what your special contribution may be.

Sharing Work

When I was in college, I had the opportunity to sing in several concerts with the San Francisco Symphony. I love choral singing for the very reason that my individual effort is lost in a sea of sound. I have only an amateur voice, but in those concerts I made the greatest musical expression I ever hope to attain. It wasn't because of my efforts; I do not even know whether I sang well or badly. But I was part of wonderful music made by a first-rate choir and orchestra. I had a part so small as to be unidentifiable, but nonetheless an active part. The work surpassed and surrounded me.

You are invited to that kind of work. You may not stand out. Your contribution may seem insignificant. Your individual achievement, though, is not the point. Ultimately everything should point away from you and toward Jesus. He is working every day. He wants you to join him, and you will learn to know him deeply as you do the work side by side in his family business.

8

Appreciation

I want to take up one final key to a personal relationship: appreciation, which makes the difference between a wary, distant relationship and one that is warm and close.

I am thinking about critical parents. My wife's father was a fine and honorable man who deeply loved Popie. He wanted the best for her and he worried over her. But he had high standards, which he applied relentlessly. Criticism took over the conversation very quickly. He found it difficult to express praise or appreciation. He wanted a close, appreciative relationship with his daughter as much as anything in the world, I suspect. He rarely experienced it, though. There was a tragic disconnect between his deep love and his inability to express appreciation.

I know many cases like that, in which parents and children keep their distance despite great love. No question, critical parents can produce wonderful children who rise to their parents' high standards. But the children get a knot in their stomach whenever they meet the parent. They keep their distance or they fight for independence. Both sides may long for easy intimacy, but they don't find it.

Many people relate to God that way. They see him as a critical parent who always expects better behavior than they can manage. As a result, he is constantly disappointed with the results they produce. Such people can't imagine God appreciating them (though he does) and they find it hard to freely appreciate him. They may have a personal relationship with God, but they are not close.

Appreciation makes all the difference—a simple activity that makes a profound impact.

When I think of appreciation, my mother comes to mind. So many times she told me—the slump-shouldered, scowling, pimpled teenager—"You look so nice when you smile." She had high standards, but her appreciation far outweighed her reproof. She thought I was a wonderful child (and thought my siblings were too); I never had a moment's doubt about that, because she told me.

My father's appreciation was not so verbal, but I knew he too was intensely proud of me. At my high school graduation, I gave a valedictory speech that began, "The students at Bullard High live under the iron hand of oppression." It got worse from there. My views were somewhat radical for their time, and afterward the adults in my life didn't quite know what to say to me. But as soon as my father saw me he said, "You have an excellent grasp of the English language." He meant it. He was always proud of his kids.

Learning about Affirmation

While my parents' appreciation contributed to a healthy and secure relationship between us, it was one-sided. I loved them, but it never occurred to me to affirm them as they affirmed me. I was not a very warm adolescent. I had deep feelings for people, but I did not know how to voice them. It was not until I had been an adult for some time that I began to learn the power of affirmation in relationships. After that I got much closer to my parents.

I learned about affirmation from the woman who became my wife. She and a circle of friends blew the cover off my guarded words. When they saw something they liked in someone, they just said it. They showed appreciation with hugs and smiles. They were so free and warm some people didn't know how to take it. But everyone who came into their circle was delighted.

I could see stiffness and cynicism falling off others as they fumbled to acknowledge the compliments given to them. I saw their lives begin to open up and respond. For the first time, I realized that affirming words were more than a social grace. They had the power to change lives and change relationships. I felt them changing mine.

I felt affirmation opening up windows in me that had long ago stuck shut. The windows creaked and balked at opening, then let blue sky and warm, fresh air into long-darkened rooms. Almost without my realizing it, a response was awakened. I began to do my own share of affirmation. One friend told me he was quite startled at the bloom of compliments, hugs, and pats from me.

Appreciation is infectious. It can spread from one person to another and through a whole community. But somebody has to start it.

God's Language

It is God who starts it. He has a world of love for his children; he sees our worth, and he affirms it. We don't have to look hard in Scripture to learn that we are valued a great deal in his eyes.

God is not like a parent who can see no fault in his children or who puts a gold star on everything they do, however juvenile. He has high standards. When you read the Bible you find plenty of stern words about our failings.

They are framed by confident hope, however. God not only expects the best from his children, he can see it coming. His affirming words spring from his relationship to us and his confidence that in company with him we will do wonderful things. He uses the words of a parent or a coach who sees potential beginning to take shape.

"I Made You"

Nobody knows your potential as much as the one who designed your life and made you from scratch.

> *For you created my inmost being;*
> *you knit me together in my mother's womb.*
> *I praise you because I am fearfully and*
> *wonderfully made;*
> *your works are wonderful,*
> *I know that full well. (Psalm 139:13– 14)*

"I Chose You"

Remember the agony of choosing teams when you were in elementary school? How you waited, wondering whether you would be chosen? You are wanted. You are chosen.

I no longer call you servants, because a servant does not know his master's business. Instead, I have called you friends, for everything that I learned from my Father I have made known to you. You did not choose me, but I chose you and appointed you to go and bear fruit—fruit that will last. Then the Father will give you whatever you ask in my name. (John 15:15– 16)

"I Sacrifice for You"

God's great esteem for us shows in his willingness to do anything to redeem us—even to give up his own life on our behalf.

Since you are precious and honored in my sight, and because I love you, I will give men in exchange for you, and people in exchange for your life. Do not be afraid, for I am with you. (Isaiah 43:4– 5)

For he chose us in him before the creation of the world to be holy and blameless in his sight. In love he predestined us to be adopted as his children through Jesus Christ, in accordance with his pleasure and will.... In him we have redemption through his blood, the forgiveness of sins, in accordance with the riches of God's grace that he lavished on us.... (Ephesians 1:4– 8)

As you read the Bible, going from the Old Testament to the New, you find more and more that words of criticism and tears of frustration dry up. More and more you read words of hope and joy. Because Jesus suffered the penalty for our failings, there is little point in emphasizing our sins. They no longer need threaten the heart of our relationship with God.

When he looks at us, our Father sees Jesus. Through Jesus he made us; in Jesus he chose us and sacrificed for us. God has done everything possible for our welfare, and now he seeks to tell us how much he loves us and what great things he expects to see in us. His words are not the unrelenting criticism and high standards of a critical parent. They encourage and affirm us.

The Spoiled Child

One of the ugliest sights in the world is the spoiled child who answers his parents' love with indifference or spite. They lavish attention on him; he shrugs and ignores them—or scowls and yells at them to leave him alone.

Some people are like that with God. Despite all he has given them, they shrug it off and demand more. They aren't grateful and they don't express thanks. They refuse to accept his encouragement and affirmation. Oddly enough, they may crave intimacy with God.

They may plead for it; they may demand it! As long as they can't respond to God's goodness with appreciation and praise, though, they will never experience a close relationship. In a healthy relationship, appreciation has to flow in both directions.

Most of us have to be taught how. Just as I had to learn how to affirm other people from my wife's example, so I had to learn to express my appreciation for God.

You can learn it in church. Worship services are like rehearsals—you are learning how to do this important activity that you will do forever. The music, the place, the approach can help you relax and forget yourself, focusing on God. The prayers and the songs are usually designed to give you experience in speaking appreciatively to God. The fact that other people are doing it with you makes it easier, I think. You feel less self-conscious if you're not the only one.

But it's possible to go to church and not get the lesson. Some people go through the motions of praising God on Sunday morning, but they don't acquire the habit deep in their souls. They are like people who put on great manners when they meet somebody important, but at home they are rude and ungracious. Appreciation for God should fill us all hours of the day and night, spilling over at random moments because we are full of its joy.

This worshipful appreciation doesn't just consist of words; it is a whole-body response. The best example may be David's behavior when the ark of the covenant came into Jerusalem. He threw off his heavy royal robes and danced like a common fool through the streets of the city. He was so happy, so grateful to God that he couldn't sit somberly like a king; he had to dance.

I find it difficult to express myself that freely. I fear looking silly—even to myself. Like a boy summoned to kiss his aunt, I become suddenly shy and uncomfortable. I feel vulnerable to other people's opinions.

Somebody is always ready to criticize. When David danced, his wife, Michal, sneered at him. "How the king of Israel has distinguished himself today, disrobing in the sight of the slave girls of his servants as any vulgar fellow would!"

He answered her in memorable words: "It is before the Lord, who chose me.... I will celebrate before the Lord. I will become even more undignified than this, and I will be humiliated in my own eyes" (2 Samuel 6:20–22). He was willing to humiliate himself on one condition: he did it before the Lord.

The Art of Praise

You get no credit for acting like a fool. The art of praise is not to out-emote others, to raise your hands higher, to dance with more reckless abandon than anybody, to roll your eyes and clap your hands. None of that will do you the least bit of good if it is done for other people's benefit. The art of praise is to get your eyes off yourself and onto God, so that you do not care how you look.

The only way to learn this is to practice it. I've already mentioned church as a kind of learning center for appreciating God. You also can learn at home.

When you open your eyes in the morning, before you rush off to work or school, take one minute to say thank you to God. You've lived through the night and another day stretches ahead of you. Life is a gift. Remember each morning to say thanks.

You can extend that into many minutes of "counting your blessings." When you're on a walk or driving in the car, see how many reasons for thankfulness you can total up. For each one say, "Thank you. You're wonderful."

We've already discussed listening and talking to God in chapters three and four. Here I'm insisting that you pay attention to a particular kind of talk—mutual appreciation. When you read the Bible, listen attentively to how God honors you—how much he cares for you, how precious he considers you. And in your prayers, make sure to make time for thanks and appreciation—for praise.

You can become more articulate and more thoughtful in your praise by reading the Psalms. They are designed to teach you how to appreciate God. Take your time with them; don't rush, but rather let the words soak in. Read them all—don't just skip to "the good ones." Some of the less attractive Psalms might grow on you and teach you a different way of appreciating God.

There's such a thing as skillful appreciation. Many people have a repertoire of about three compliments: "You look terrific," "Your hair is great," "You are so funny." But other people say appreciative comments that inspire you with their insight. They're deep. They express an appreciation of character attributes that nobody has ever verbalized. They're gracefully expressed.

The Psalms—and all the Scriptures—express appreciation for God in wonderful poetic language. They offer insight into God's character and his work. You can learn a lot about God by reading the Psalms. Don't read them to yourself. Read them aloud to God.

Three Ways of Praise

Praise in the Psalms speaks in three different modes, each important. They all have to do with who God is and what he does.

You Are the Creator

You made the world and you made me—and I am so very thankful. The beauty of the earth, of the creatures, of the skies are all reasons to thank God. All the gifts of life are reasons to appreciate God.

You Are the Judge

Amid all the competing factions of our world—the bullies and victims, the screams and tears—God alone knows all. He is able to untangle all the complications and see the truth. He brings people to justice. He lifts up the weak and poor. He brings the wicked to account. Fairness is coming. We get impatient because it doesn't come on our schedule. Only God, however, is competent and worthy to judge the world. All that is worthy of our praise.

You Are the Redeemer

More than any other subject, this is the heart of praise. God rescues people who are desperate. When the Psalms take up this subject—and they often do—they remember again and again the way God saved Israel when they were helpless slaves in Egypt. When the early Christians began to praise God for what they had experienced, they added a second exodus—God's rescue of his people when they were helpless slaves to sin.

Appreciation

Left to ourselves, most of us would thank God for the things he did for us individually. He kept us safe on an icy road. He brought a man or woman to marry into our life. He helped us get out of a jam after we prayed in desperation.

That's fine as a starting place. But God wants us to expand our understanding so we can appreciate the really great things he has done for everyone. Because when we appreciate these, we are appreciating him on his terms. We are understanding his whole character, not just the part that touches us today. That is a much bigger base on which to build a strong personal relationship.

In a healthy, loving relationship, mutual appreciation is no more remarkable than eating breakfast. People who are close do it constantly, almost without thinking. They love to speak out loud their appreciation —because they love the person they are speaking to.

Your relationship with God should be like that. You get a daily dose of his appreciation for you. You speak a daily dose of your appreciation for him. Occasionally, you go further and pour yourself into praise. You might get quite emotional at times. The greatest emotions, though, are those of the everyday. You love God and you tell him so. He does the same to you. That's how it is in close personal relationships.

9

Face-to-Face

So, is it really possible to have a personal relationship with God?

Yes, it is.

As I look back over more than forty years of following Jesus, I recall plenty of doubts and dark nights. But I also see a steady, comforting, and very personal relationship—a journey in company with a God I can relate to. He is not a vague or distant presence. I know him, and he knows me. I talk to him, calling him by name. He talks to me. I know his family. I share his work. We affirm each other. In times of suffering, we are particularly close because he knows how I feel. This relationship is as inescapably real as any of my relationships.

But it is not perfect. I can't see him.

No matter how sophisticated we become, at our simplest and most emotional level we long to see God.

Little children ask, "How big is God?" and "What does God look like?" until parents and teachers warn them away from such questions. But none of us ever totally shakes the feeling that some dark night we will rise out of bed to see God coming.

In *Out of Africa* Isak Dinesen tells a story of her Kenyan cook Kamante:

> One night, after midnight, he [Kamante] suddenly walked into my bedroom with a hurricane-lamp in his hand, silent, as if on duty. It must have been only a short time after he came into my house, for he was very small; he stood by my bedside like a dark bat that had strayed into the room, with very big spreading ears, or like a small African Will-o'-the-wisp, with his lamp in his hand. He spoke to me very solemnly, "Msabu," he said, "I think you had better get up." I sat up in bed bewildered; I thought that if anything serious had happened, it would have been Farah who would have come to fetch me, but when I told Kamante to go away again, he did not move. "Msabu," he said again, "I think that you had better get up. I think that God is coming." When I heard this, I did get up, and asked why he thought so. He gravely led me into the dining-room which looked West, toward the hills. From the door-windows I now saw a strange phenomenon. There was a big grass-fire

going on, out in the hills, and the grass burning all the way from the hill-top to the plain; when seen from the house it was nearly a vertical line. It did indeed look as if some gigantic figure was moving and coming toward us. I stood for some time and looked at it, with Kamante watching by my side, then I began to explain the thing to him. I meant to quiet him for I thought that he had been terribly frightened. But the explanation did not seem to make much impression on him one way or the other; he clearly took his mission to have been fulfilled when he called me. "Well yes," he said, "it may be so. But I thought that you had better get up in case it was God coming."

Indeed, such a thought can frighten us in the middle of the night. It can also touch something deeply hungry inside us.

The Benefits of Sight

"Seeing is believing," we say, and though we know we must walk by faith, not by sight, it would be easier to believe if we could see God. To see God is to know that he is real.

But seeing is more than mere proof of existence. When I go away on a business trip I never doubt that my wife exists. Nor do I doubt that she loves me and is faithful to me. At any moment I can pick up a phone and talk to her. Yet my eyes remain hungry for the sight of her.

While I am away I may ask someone, "Would you like to see my family?" I pull out little rectangles of colored paper on which replicas of the faces of my wife and children are printed. Of course you cannot really see my wife and children. The rectangles of paper are mere representations of their actual faces. A complex machine recorded the pattern of light emanating from their faces; another machine read the digital rendering of those patterns and duplicated them on paper using tiny dots of ink. My little wallet-sized colored rectangles are quite unlike my family. Yet looking at those photographs while I am traveling, I long to be with them; I feel a moment of communion, a painful communion of absence and longing. And I show the rectangles to my friends, confident that somehow something of my wife and children will be communicated.

We want to see; we never feel satisfied in a relationship when we cannot. Anyone who has carried on an acquaintance purely over the phone or through an Internet chat knows what I'm talking about. There is a dimension of each other you can never quite grasp. And when you already know each other by sight—as in the case of my wife—the phone only accentuates your sense of absence. I long for her touch, her scent. But most of all I long to see her face.

The scientist and philosopher Michael Polanyi noted that in a crowded station, with thousands of people, he could unfailingly recognize his wife's face. No close resemblance would ever fool him; in a million tries he would never be wrong. And yet if he sent someone else to meet his wife, he could never adequately describe her face. Someone who had never seen her would be at a near-total loss in trying to find her, no matter how carefully her appearance had been detailed.

We know faces by sight; our brains are wired to remember them. They represent the unique person as no other part of the body—hands or feet—can ever do.

No wonder that when the Bible speaks of longing for God, it speaks in terms of his face. The psalmist pleads with God, "Make your face shine upon us," and "Do not hide your face from us." David's heart urges him to "seek God's face." And ultimately, he says, "in righteousness I will see your face; when I awake, I will be satisfied with seeing your likeness" (Psalm 17:15).

Such language came effortlessly even though, as Jews, they believed making any image of God's face to be blasphemy. They longed not just for God's blessings, they longed for God himself. And at some primitive, urgent level, "him" was his face.

God Has a Face

Jesus is God, and he has a face. His disciples knew that face the way they knew their wives' faces—out of a million tries they would identify him every time. Interestingly, they made no attempt to pass on any physical description.

Ever since, artists have been intrigued by the challenge. Rembrandt, out of them all, focused his interest on Jesus' face. His portraits of Jesus are compelling—deep, searching, compassionate eyes. But of course, they are not really a record of what Jesus looked like. They are more a record of what Rembrandt's faith looked like.

Jesus is gone, and we are left still longing to see God. Yet in one very important way we are in a different position from people who came before Jesus. Though we do not see God's face, we now know that he has one. If Jesus is "the image of the invisible God," as his disciples proclaimed, then we know that God has a face.

He is not a force. He is not a principle. He is not anything like an ocean into which we will disappear. When God reveals himself he has a face. And that means, surely, we can have a personal relationship with him. In fact, we must. If we do not have a personal relationship with him, we do not know him in the way he wants to be known.

We are promised someday to see him face-to-face (1 Corinthians 13:12). Until then, we are like people whose closest friend is on a journey. We know him. We can talk to him. We can partner with him in the work he is doing. When we suffer we can share with him our deepest feelings. But we cannot see him, and we miss him.

Absence is hard on a relationship. Early in the Iraq war, I talked to an army chaplain who had just come back from the war zone. We were attending a conference on "Smart Marriages," and I asked him how the war affected families. When he first arrived in Iraq, he told me, his commander asked him whether he had been down to the phone banks to listen to the soldiers calling their families. The chaplain was taken aback by the question. "We can't listen in on phone conversations," he said. His commander told him to go to the telephones and he would understand.

The phone banks were open-air installations, dozens of telephones made available to the fighting forces to call home. You did not need to tap the lines to know what the soldiers were saying, the chaplain said. Many were shouting angrily into the telephones, trying to get their wives or husbands to do what they wanted them to do. The stress of combat and a long absence was putting great strain on some of those marriages.

"Absence makes the heart grow fonder," we say, and it can be true. But absence may also break people apart, which makes Jesus' prayer for us all the more poignant. He knew that he would be absent in body for a very long time and that we would miss him. So he prayed for us in advance: "My prayer is not for [my disciples] alone. I pray also for those who will believe in me through their message, that all of them may be one, Father, just as you are in me and I am in you. May they also be in us ... I in them and you in me" (John 17:20–23).

It is for personal relationship that Jesus prays—close personal relationship. He wants us to have the closeness to each other that he and his Father experience. He wants us to be "in" God and he wants to be "in" us. Despite the pain of absence, he asks the Father to create the closest personal relationships—with each other and with God.

What, Really, Is the Problem?

It is no accident that many people make their best life-long friends while they are young and have uncrowded hours to spend together—almost unlimited time. When will we again have time like the days of childhood, when we played together from dawn to dusk? When will we again have time like high school or college, when we sat up late at night and talked? Those friendships endure beyond school because we keep piling more time on top of our initial investment.

It takes time to know other people. A mind like Einstein's may master calculus in a day, but it cannot by the same pure power master another human life. You cannot plow through a person's character the way a graduate student plows through his subject at the library. Human lives, being fragile, characteristically hide. Only love, patiently applied over time, can bring them out. Only a lifetime of love can understand them.

We need unlimited time to grasp God. If certain theologians are right and eternity is a timeless state, a beyond-time in which a changeless God lives and contains all the changes of time, then we can imagine (faintly) the continuous rolling over of knowledge we will experience there. We will discover and rediscover and joyfully discover again the many facets of our infinitely splendid God. Everything about him will be ever new, never routine, always a delightful shock. "It is really true," we will say. "I am really here, and so is he."

Eternity starts now. That is what John's gospel promises when it says that "whoever believes in the

Son has eternal life" (John 3:36). The time I have been given here and now leads into eternity.

God has given us time to know him. Hebrews refers to God's time as Today: "Today, if you hear his voice, do not harden your hearts" (4:7). We have to give God our Today. The problem is not lack of opportunity. The problem is in our hearts.

My Aversion to God

My problem with a personal relationship with God is my deep residual aversion to God, my lack of faith, which keeps me from taking the opportunities I have. He is not hiding from me; I hide from him.

When I was in college I said to God, in some desperation, "If you would just show yourself to me, show me that you are unquestionably and absolutely real, I would be able to love you forever without any question." God knows that was pure self-deception on my part. Every time he has shown himself to men and women they have gone off in some other direction. They have gloried in the momentary splendor of his presence and then stubbornly wandered off on their own. Am I any different?

I confess my faith in God, that he deserves my complete adoration and obedience. But when I wake in the morning, other realities are on my mind. I do not jump out of bed eager to talk with him. I have my mind on a shower, on breakfast, on work—not on his presence.

In Romans, Paul summarizes my double-minded dilemma. "So then, I myself in my mind am a slave to God's law, but in the sinful nature a slave to the law of sin" (7:25). What can I do about this? Paul's answer is twofold.

The first, great overwhelming answer is that I can and need do nothing about it; only Jesus can and does rescue me. I am forgiven because of his death on the cross. "There is now no condemnation for those who are in Christ Jesus" (8:1). "[Nothing] will be able to separate us from the love of God that is in Christ Jesus our Lord" (8:39).

The second answer—a small one compared to the first—is that I must respond to God as I am able. I can overcome my aversion day by day because God will enable me to do so. "We have an obligation—but it is not to the sinful nature, to live according to it. For if you live according to the sinful nature, you will die; but if by the Spirit you put to death the misdeeds of the body, you will live, because those who are led by the Spirit of God are sons of God" (8:12–14). To live as a child of God, in a living, breathing relationship to him,

I must turn to him and, helped by his living presence, stop living by sin and begin living by his life.

James puts it this way: "Come near to God and he will come near to you" (James 4:8). The only cure for my residual aversion to God is to move toward him, to spend time with him by the means he has offered. As David said, "Taste and see that the Lord is good." When I taste, the sweetness increases my appetite for more.

I must apply this cure again and again. I slip back into forgetfulness. God is easy to put aside because he is out of sight. He has gone to prepare a place for me, and he has been gone a long time. I miss him. Sometimes I forget him.

Yet like Paul, "I want to know Christ and the power of his resurrection and the fellowship of sharing in his sufferings.... Not that I have already obtained all this, or have already been made perfect, but I press on to take hold of that for which Christ Jesus took hold of me. Brothers, I do not consider myself yet to have taken hold of it. But one thing I do: Forgetting what is behind and straining toward what is ahead, I press on" (Philippians 3:10–14).

God has introduced himself and offered a personal relationship. We must take him up on the offer, with all we have to give.

The Bride of Christ

In the Bible, Paul refers to the church as the "bride of Christ" (Ephesians 5:23) whom Jesus loves and cherishes. The marriage of Jesus and his church is usually interpreted as something complete. I think it would be more accurate, however, to say that this marriage is in process—that we are engaged to Christ and waiting for the wedding.

I hasten to add that a first-century Jewish engagement was nothing tentative. For a Jewish couple in those days, engagement was as firm a commitment as marriage. In fact it was the same commitment. The man had paid the marriage price in the presence of witnesses. She was even called his wife. The engagement could not be broken except through the same provisions as for a divorce. Unfaithfulness during the engagement was considered adultery and punished as such. In the eyes of others the engaged couple were husband and wife. The only reservation was that they did not live or sleep together. In that sense—an important sense!—the engagement period was a time of waiting for the celebration and consummation.

We are with Jesus in that engagement period. We are absolutely committed to life together—we committed to Jesus, he committed to us. But we have not yet reached our goal.

There is a special tenderness and closeness during engagement. I remember this from my own. Popie and I knew we were in a passing stage. Something much better was going to happen to us, something we looked forward to passionately. Yet we knew we were going to get there, and get there together. We were very much in love.

Seen with Jewish eyes, this waiting period is especially sweet. Oriental fathers kept their marriageable daughters secluded from the world. A young girl might not even see her prospective husband until they were actually engaged. Then, once the commitments were made, they were allowed a wondrous, unprecedented privilege. Now they could meet, talk, hold hands, walk together. Those times must have seemed like an incredible, joyful freedom.

Inevitably, the initial joy would wear off, and both would feel some frustration as they waited for the wedding day. It's natural. Anticipation is part of celebration.

I recall my intense desire to be with Popie. I was oblivious to other people and circumstances, because my thoughts were focused on her. I wanted to know all about her. The days were never long enough for us, because we wanted so much to be together and to learn about each other. No longer were we just trying out a relationship to see how we would like it. Now we were building it.

So are we with Jesus. We are building a relationship that will carry on forever, deeper and holier and love-lier every year now and forever. He is a personal God. He relates to us personally. He is our friend. He loves us. He will never let go of us. We can know him. And amazingly wonderful joy is yet to come.

I value your thoughts about what you've just read.
Please share them with me. You'll find contact information
in the back of this book.

Acknowledgment

My special thanks to John Sloan, who first saw the potential of this book, convinced me of it, advocated its cause with others, and encouraged me until it was done. He is not only an outstanding editor, he is a faithful friend.

Share Your Thoughts

With the Author: Your comments will be forwarded to
the author when you send them to *zauthor@zondervan.com*.

With Zondervan: Submit your review of this book
by writing to *zreview@zondervan.com*.

Free Online Resources at
www.zondervan.com/hello

 Zondervan AuthorTracker: Be notified whenever your
favorite authors publish new books, go on tour, or post
an update about what's happening in their lives.

 Daily Bible Verses and Devotions: Enrich your life
with daily Bible verses or devotions that help you start
every morning focused on God.

 Free Email Publications: Sign up for newsletters on
fiction, Christian living, church ministry, parenting, and
more.

 Zondervan Bible Search: Find and compare
Bible passages in a variety of translations at
www.zondervanbiblesearch.com.

 Other Benefits: Register yourself to receive online
benefits like coupons and special offers, or to participate
in research.